THE MEMOIRS OF ERNEST A. FORSSGREN

THE MEMOIRS OF

Ernest A. Forssgren

PROUST'S SWEDISH VALET

❖ ❖ ❖

EDITED AND ANNOTATED BY

William C. Carter

YALE UNIVERSITY PRESS
NEW HAVEN & LONDON

Published with assistance from the foundation established in memory of Philip Hamilton McMillan of the Class of 1894, Yale College.

All illustrations are courtesy of the Marcel Proust Collection at the Mervyn H. Sterne Library, the University of Alabama at Birmingham.

Designed by James J. Johnson and set in Fairfield Medium type by The Composing Room of Michigan, Inc.
Printed in the United States of America by Sheridan Books, Inc.

Library of Congress Cataloging-in-Publication Data
Forssgren, Ernest A., 1894–1970.
    The memoirs of Ernest A. Forssgren, Proust's Swedish valet / edited and annotated by William C. Carter.
        p.   cm.
    Includes bibliographical references and index.
    ISBN-13: 978-0-300-11463-8 (cloth : alk. paper)
    ISBN-10: 0-300-11463-X (cloth : alk. paper)
    1. Proust, Marcel, 1871–1922—Relations with valets.   2. Forssgren, Ernest A., 1894–1970.   I. Carter, William C.   II. Title.
    PQ2631.R63Z5973 2006
    843'.912—dc22

                                                                    2005028454

A catalogue record for this book is available from the British Library.

The paper in this book meets the guidelines for permanence and durability of the Committee on Production Guidelines for Book Longevity of the Council on Library Resources.

10 9 8 7 6 5 4 3 2 1

For Marilyn Gordon, who made this book possible

Contents

❖ ❖ ❖

Preface

❖   ❖   ❖

A few years ago, when I was invited to St. Louis to speak about my biography *Marcel Proust: A Life,* Marilyn Gordon, who lives nearby, read a newspaper article about my lecture. This reminded her that she had material related to Proust that had been given to her many years earlier by Ernest Forssgren, an old family friend who, in his youth, had served briefly as Proust's valet. Marilyn Gordon contacted me and asked whether I would be interested in seeing the Proust items, which she had never shown to anyone outside the family. I leave it to you to imagine my eager reply.

We met the following day and had a lively discussion about Proust and Forssgren. The memoirs and memorabilia brought to me by Ms. Gordon provide new and interesting details about the Proust-Forssgren connection, as well as new information about Albert Le Cuziat, who was a primary source for Proust for information about genealogy and protocol in Parisian high society, as well as scandalous information about the sexual predilections of prominent Parisians.

Marilyn Gordon generously donated the Forssgren memoirs and the Proust memorabilia to the Marcel Proust Collection at the Mervyn H. Sterne Library of the University of Alabama at Birmingham (UAB). The donation, consisting of documents previously unknown, includes two autograph items:

1. A signed copy of the first edition (1913) of *Du côté de chez Swann* (*Swann's Way*), the first volume of Proust's multivolume novel *À la recherche du temps perdu* (formerly known in English as *Remembrance of Things Past,* in current editions *In Search of Lost Time*).

2. An inscribed photograph of Proust seated on a divan. This photo was made at Otto's studio, where fashionable Parisians often went to have their pictures taken.

The other items are:

3. A telegram Proust sent Forssgren in 1922.

4. A two-page, single-spaced statement that Forssgren wrote in response to publication in 1965 of the second and final volume of George D. Painter's biography (*Proust: The Later Years*).

5. A copy of Painter's second volume belonging to Forssgren, which contains notations on the end papers and on the pages of the book.

6. The typescript of Forssgren's ninety-three-page memoirs, written in English, which include a description of his first encounter with Proust in 1914 and his last attempts to see Proust in 1922. He also recounts his early years in America as a valet and would-be inventor. The existence of these memoirs has been known since 1975, when a small portion of

them was excerpted and published in French in the
Études proustiennes.

7. A copy of Forssgren's proposed phonetic alphabet to
reform the spelling of the English language.

8. A photograph of Ernest Forssgren in his later years.

Acknowledgments

❖   ❖   ❖

I would like to thank the following people for their invaluable assistance and encouragement in the editing and annotating of the Forssgren documents: Bob Borson; Robert Blumenfeld; Elyane Dezon-Jones; Karen J. Downs; J. P. Smith; Roy Shigley; the late Dr. L. M. Bargeron Jr., Henrik Vitalis, archivist of the Church of Sweden; Liz Steinberg, archivist, Duke Farms Foundation; Elizabeth Donn, research services librarian, Duke University; Caroline Szylowicz, Kolb-Proust Librarian at the Kolb-Proust Archive for Research, University of Illinois Library; Bert Lippincott, librarian, Newport Historical Society; Steven G. Drexler, forensic document examiner, Department of Forensics, University of Alabama at Birmingham; my friends and colleagues at Mervyn H. Sterne Library, University of Alabama at Birmingham; my editors at Yale University Press, John Kulka and Dan Heaton; and, especially, my wife, Lynn.

Abbreviations of Titles of Proust's Works

❖ ❖ ❖

All quotations from *In Search of Lost Time* are from the Modern Library Edition in six volumes, translated by C. K. Scott Moncrieff and Terence Kilmartin, revised by D. J. Enright, New York, 1992. Each section of the novel is cited by its title, volume number, and page number:

1 *Swann's Way*
2 *Within a Budding Grove*
3 *The Guermantes Way*
4 *Sodom and Gomorrah*
5 *The Captive* and *The Fugitive*
6 *Time Regained*

The following abbreviations are used for the correspondence of Marcel Proust:

Corr.: Correspondance de Marcel Proust, edited by Philip Kolb. Paris: Plon, 21 vols., 1970–93.

SL 1: Selected Letters in English, 1880–1903, edited by Philip Kolb, translated by Ralph Manheim, introduction by J. M. Cocking. New York: Doubleday, 1983.

SL 2: Selected Letters, 1904–1909, vol. 2, edited by Philip Kolb, translated with an introduction by Terence Kilmartin. London, 1989.

SL 3: Selected Letters, 1910–1917, vol. 3, edited by Philip Kolb, translated with an introduction by Terence Kilmartin. New York: HarperCollins, 1992.

SL 4: Selected Letters, 1918–1922, vol. 4, edited by Philip Kolb, translated with an introduction by Joanna Kilmartin. London: HarperCollins, 2000.

For those works and documents that exist only in French, all translations are my own unless otherwise indicated.

THE MEMOIRS OF ERNEST A. FORSSGREN

Ernest Forssgren

❖ ❖ ❖

ERNEST Forssgren was born in 1894, in northern Sweden, to a large, respectable, and religious family of
modest means.[1] The only detail that he provides
about his family's circumstances is that his parents were
struggling to send a son—presumably the eldest—through
Uppsala University. The financial strains the family endured
forced Ernest, at the early age of thirteen, to drop out of
school, leave home, and venture forth on his own. In his late
teens, Forssgren decided to seek his fortune in another country and went to London for a short time, then to Paris.

Although Forssgren appeared in Proust's life only briefly,

1. According to his death certificate, obtained from the state of California, Forssgren was born on June 9, 1894. Regarding his family, Forssgren
writes of brothers and sisters in the memoirs but never provides a head
count. Based on his use of the plural "sisters" and the mention of one
brother attending Uppsala University while another was working and studying in Paris, there must have been at least five children, including Ernest.

he did so at two crucial points: first in 1914 and then in 1922. In the late summer of 1914, shortly after the beginning of World War I, Forssgren served as Proust's valet during the writer's last trip to the Grand-Hôtel in Cabourg on the Normandy coast. Proust also brought along his new housekeeper Céleste Albaret. The only descriptions we have of what Forssgren was like in 1914 are Proust's brief comments, in a letter to a friend, recalling the nineteen-year-old Swede's blond good looks, and Céleste's slightly fuller but unflattering portrait, in her memoirs, regarding his personality and character. Her recollections, like Forssgren's, were written more than half a century after Proust's death.

In the spring of 1915, with Proust's encouragement, Forssgren decided to emigrate to the United States to avoid being drafted into the Swedish army. In 1922, using money earned from a patent, Forssgren came back to Sweden to visit his family for the first time since leaving home. As he relates in his memoirs, the reunion did not go well. Forssgren decided to return to New York by way of Paris, primarily to renew his acquaintance with Proust, a man he says he worshiped and who had, Forssgren claims, promised to help advance his career as a teacher and writer. The two men tried unsuccessfully to meet. This missed encounter produced several documents: a note left at Forssgren's hotel by Proust, who had stopped by unannounced hoping to catch him in; a telegram, previously unknown, from Proust to Forssgren; and a letter. Of these, only the recently discovered telegram survives. The telegram helps to establish with greater precision the chronology of Proust's final months and pushes back somewhat earlier than previously believed the date of the missed rendezvous at the Riviera Hotel, an event that Forssgren, to his horror, believed was the indirect cause of the novelist's demise. Of the note Proust left at the hotel, we have only a photocopy; a portion of the letter survives, also in photo-copy.

Forssgren was an amateur linguist (with the emphasis on amateur), a fierce Anglophobe (the result of his brief stay in London), and an unsuccessful inventor. It will be obvious to the reader of his memoirs that the handsome young Swede held a high opinion of himself and was extremely self-confident, even to the point of trying to undertake a reform of the English language. In a number of episodes, elements of which border on the improbable, Forssgren eagerly casts himself in the role of the hero. The conflicts and misunderstandings he endures at the hands of others, usually people he considered his social inferiors, are due, he says, to their jealousy over his exceptional qualities and superior intellect. Ultimately, by his own admission, Forssgren's story is a sad one of a man who felt himself a failure and became embittered toward the end of his life. His testament, given in what he calls his "summary" of Painter, has the tone of a doomsday preacher warning of fire and brimstone. Forssgren died on November 28, 1970, in Santa Cruz, California. His last known place of residence was San Francisco.

The Job Applicant

❖ ❖ ❖

I n early September 1914, Ernest Forssgren, a nineteen-
year-old Swede, recently unemployed, crossed the Seine
and headed for 102 boulevard Haussmann.[1] Before ring-
ing the bell, he gazed at the solid stone façade, whose
wrought-iron balconies bespoke Right Bank bourgeois re-
spectability and wealth but lacked the stately grandeur of the
Russian Prince Alexis Orloff's mansion in the old aristocratic
quarter of the faubourg Saint-Germain, Forssgren's previous
place of employment.

It is unimaginable how many lives had been forever altered just a month earlier, on August 2, when the French government ordered the mobilization of the army, an action followed the next day by Germany's declaration of war on

1. The only episodes for which Forssgren's memoirs coincide with
those of Céleste Albaret are the 1914 trip to Cabourg and Proust's death.
The memoirists' respective versions of these events will be discussed in the
context of Forssgren's memoirs.

4

France. In Forssgren's case, the beginning of hostilities and the rapid advance of the German forces had sent his former employer, the wealthy, volatile Prince Orloff, speeding away in his Rolls-Royce to safety in his château in Pau, fleeing what appeared to be the imminent bombardment of Paris, followed by the German invasion of the city.

Prince Orloff's château was actually smaller than his Paris mansion, and he had left the capital with a reduced household staff. Forssgren, a fairly recent hire, was among those left behind to find a new position. The young Swede dreaded, as much as anyone else, the prospects of seeing Paris fall to the enemy. He had been in France for little more than a year, but he had quickly fallen in love with all things French, a reaction quite the opposite of his earlier experience in London, which had left him repelled by the English and their ways.

The man with the job vacancy Forssgren hoped to fill, Marcel Proust, had decided—at no matter what risk—to remain in Paris, where he had always lived. Forssgren knew nothing about his prospective employer, except that he had advertised for a valet de chambre. If domestic jobs were scarce because so many of the well-to-do had abandoned the city, applicants were even scarcer because all the able-bodied young men—and many, besides, who were neither young nor fit—had suddenly found themselves in uniform and were either at the front or occupied elsewhere in support roles for the military. Confident that he could meet the requirements of this Monsieur Proust, Forssgren rang the bell.

Céleste Albaret opened the door and showed him in. She noted that this young man appeared to be in excellent health compared with the first candidate, who had applied after being rejected by the military as unfit. That haggard youth's appearance had so appalled Proust that he described him as

"Galloping Consumption in person."[2] Forssgren did not know that Céleste had taken over the management of the household only two weeks earlier as a direct consequence of the war; Proust's manservant Nicolas Cottin and his driver Odilon Albaret, Céleste's husband, had been among the first to be drafted. For reasons of propriety, Proust had launched the vain search for a new manservant, although Céleste, to her employer's amazement and delight, had gamely offered to disguise herself as a man for Proust's annual trip to the seaside resort of Cabourg, the departure for which awaited only the hiring of a new valet.[3] In spite of Proust's long-held fascination for transvestism, he declined Céleste's surprising proposition and continued to interview job applicants, of whom there were precious few.

Forssgren found Céleste's appearance and manners so refined that he mistook her for the lady of the house. (Proust came to enjoy telling his aristocratic friends, such as the duchesse de Clermont-Tonnerre, that Céleste was "a delightful person who is the niece of the Archbishop of Tours and looks like Lady de Grey forty years ago.")[4] She asked Forssgren to wait while she informed M. Proust of his arrival.

The young Swede had no inkling that he was about to enter one of the most remarkable creative spaces in Paris: the famous cork-lined room where the sedentary author slept all day, venturing out—when he did leave his sanctuary—only late in the evening, returning to his bed to write, listening to

2. SL 3: 276.

3. On August 30, only a day or so before Forssgren showed up for the interview, Proust told his friend Reynaldo Hahn, "I think I can perfectly well take Madame Albaret to Cabourg in present circumstances; she offered to put on male clothes, which I refused, but she would impersonate very respectably some Comtesse or other." Ibid.

4. Ibid., 3: 370.

his "nocturnal muse," before switching off the light just as the immense city was waking to a new day in an atmosphere now charged with the dread and excitement of war. Forssgren might have supposed that all the windows and shutters in the apartment were closed and draped with heavy blue curtains in anticipation of blackouts, but this was not at all the reason. Proust had long since blocked out any hint of daylight and drafts of air, maintaining a kind of perpetual night in his apartment. Like the protagonist of his novel, he claimed to be so sensitive that even without the light and noises from the street, he could gauge the time of the day and the temper of the weather: "At daybreak, my face still turned to the wall, and before I had seen above the big window-curtains what shade of colour the first streaks of light assumed, I could already tell what the weather was like."[5] The perpetual nighttime in which Proust lived gave the illusion of stopping time, allowing him to pay no heed to the rising or setting sun, as he maintained a tyrannical control over a routine uniquely suited to his needs. The writer had organized his life, a friend was to say, in order to produce a masterpiece. But Proust had not yet been widely recognized as a literary genius.

Céleste returned and led Forssgren in to meet Proust. It was the novelist's custom, as the most famous valetudinarian in Paris, to receive male visitors while he lay in bed, propped up on pillows. As Forssgren followed Céleste through the apartment to Proust's room, he observed with disdain the massive, ugly bourgeois furnishings typical of the era. An atmosphere of silence and claustrophobia engulfed the youth, who already dreaded the prospect of working in such an environment, especially after having grown accustomed to the prince's spacious, airy palace, where the expatriate lad was

5. *The Captive* 5: 1.

one of a number of menservants dressed in regal livery performing his duties under the expert tutelage of the head footman, Albert Le Cuziat. But Forssgren desperately needed a job, even if it meant becoming temporarily cloistered with an obscure gentleman.

Although Proust constantly depicted himself in letters to friends as ill and confined to his bed, he had a vast reservoir of strength and will when it came to what mattered most: the making of his book. Everyone who met Proust noticed the large, almond-shaped eyes that gave the impression of totally taking one in, and Forssgren was no exception, finding the dark, languorous, absorbing eyes to be the author's "most striking feature." Marie Scheikévitch, who had met Proust a few years earlier at one of Madeleine Lemaire's musical evenings, found his gaze "so penetrating that it was evident one was confronting a pitiless observer."[6] No one who saw those eyes ever forgot being caught in their stare.

The eight months before Forssgren rang the bell at boulevard Haussmann had been the most dramatic in Proust's life. He had experienced a touch of personal triumph in November 1913, when after years of false starts and failures, he had published, albeit at his own expense, *Swann's Way,* the thick first volume of *In Search of Lost Time,* which promised to be the longest, most complex novel ever written. To the surprise of many, including the three now-chagrined publishers who had rejected the manuscript, the book was enjoying success, and many whose opinions counted for something had hailed the author as a vibrant new voice.

On November 21, 1913, a week after the publication of *Swann's Way,* the composer Reynaldo Hahn had written to

6. Marie Scheikévitch, *Time Past: Memories of Proust and Others* (Boston: Houghton Mifflin, 1935), 154.

Madame Joseph Duglé, Charles Gounod's niece, to express an opinion about *Swann's Way* and make a prediction: "Proust's book is not a masterpiece if by masterpiece one means a *perfect* thing with an *irreproachable design*. But it is without a doubt (and here my friendship plays no part) *the finest book* to appear since [Gustave Flaubert's] *l'Éducation sentimentale*. From *the first line* a *great genius* reveals itself, and since this opinion one day will be universal, we must get used to it at once." Hahn refuted the widely held notion that Proust was merely a socialite and literary lightweight: "It's always difficult to get it into your head that someone whom you meet in society is a genius. And yet Stendhal, Chateaubriand, and Vigny went out in society a great deal."[7]

Proust, however, had not been able to savor to the fullest his literary vindication. Within six months of publication, two tragedies that touched him closely had largely spoiled his joy at seeing his work finally in print and in the hands of admiring readers. On March 16, 1914, his good friend Gaston Calmette, editor of *Le Figaro*, one of France's leading newspapers, had been murdered at his desk by the outraged wife of a leading politician whose corrupt policies the journalist had been exposing in the newspaper. On learning, late in the evening, of Calmette's murder, Proust had rushed to his office at *Le Figaro* "with a feeling of dread and the need to see once more that corridor along which he escorted me so often and that frightful woman followed him."[8]

Calmette, perhaps more than anyone, certainly more than any publisher, had encouraged Proust's career by printing in *Le Figaro* many of his articles, essays, and parodies. He had also attempted to help find a publisher for *In Search of*

7. *Corr.* 12: 333. The emphasis is Hahn's.
8. *SL* 3: 236.

Lost Time and had even promised to serialize the first volume in the newspaper, until he learned its extraordinary length. He then attempted to persuade other publishers to bring out the volume. Although all these efforts came to naught, Proust remained loyal to Calmette. As a New Year's gift—but mainly to thank him for his failed efforts to secure a publisher— Proust had Tiffany's make Calmette "a black moiré cigarette-case with a monogram in brilliants."[9] And, later in the year, as he had always intended, Proust dedicated *Swann's Way* to Calmette, "as a token of profound and affectionate gratitude." The journalist, apparently too distracted by the political storm he was helping to create, never thanked Proust for the cigarette case or the dedication.

Proust was still mourning Calmette's death when Alfred Agostinelli, his beloved secretary, was killed in an airplane crash off the coast of Antibes on May 30. Not only was the author bereaved, he felt guilty over the young man's death. Just six months earlier, in order to escape the constraints of the writer's infatuation with him, Agostinelli and his common-law wife, Anna, who had been residing in Proust's apartment, had packed their bags and sneaked out of the building. Believing rightly that Proust would stop at nothing to secure Agostinelli's return, the couple fled to the Riviera, where Alfred intended to pursue his career as a pilot.

When Forssgren arrived for the interview, Proust's household, like most others in Paris, was in something of a turmoil. In spite of the German advance toward Paris, the writer intended to leave for his annual summer vacation on the coast at Cabourg if the trains were running and if he could find a new manservant. Now, at the very last minute, a handsome, obviously healthy young man had miraculously appeared,

9. Ibid., 3: 144.

with an excellent letter of recommendation from Alex Pralon, Prince Orloff's secretary. Ernest Forssgren held ideal credentials in another way as well: as a foreigner from a neutral country, he was immune to the draft. As long as Sweden remained neutral, Forssgren need not worry about being called to arms. At forty-three, Proust was, of course, too old and too ill to be called up; but eventually, as the war wore on and the supply of men grew scarce, the government increased the age of those drafted and even he was summoned periodically to report for medical examinations.

The trip on which Forssgren accompanied Proust and Céleste was to be the writer's last to the Normandy seaside resort that had been his preferred vacation spot for seven consecutive summers. Proust managed to obtain three train tickets for Cabourg leaving on September 3.[10] On the eve of his departure, he arose one evening and went out for a walk in the capital, fearing that when he returned everything might be altered. He described the experience in a letter to a friend: "When the siege of Paris seemed imminent, I got up one evening and went out into a clear, resplendent, reproving, serene, ironic, and maternal moonlight, and seeing the immense city which I never knew I loved so much waiting in its futile beauty for the onslaught that nothing seemed capable any longer of preventing, I couldn't refrain from sobbing."[11]

In the first battle of the Marne, which began on Septem-

10. *Corr.* 13: 15. Based on Forssgren's memoirs, it seems likely that he came for the interview on September 2.

11. Ibid. 14: 71. Proust has his Narrator take a similar moonlight walk in wartime Paris and express identical sentiments; see *Time Regained* 6: 161–62. The author frequently transposed, for inclusion in the novel, his own experiences, which he sometimes first described in letters or in conversations with friends.

ber 6 and raged for three days, with both sides taking heavy casualties, the Allies succeeded in halting the German advance on Paris. Proust was to suffer the loss of friends during the war, notably the adored Count Bertrand de Fénelon, and the war significantly altered the content and dimensions of his novel.

By the time Ernest Forssgren arrived at 102 boulevard Haussmann, Marcel Proust had long since lost all his illusions about erotic love and was deeply preoccupied with transposing his knowledge of the poisonous effects of sexual jealousy, gleaned from bitter experience, into a key theme of his great novel. Although Forssgren served as Proust's valet for only a brief period, his Nordic good looks made an indelible impression. As we shall see, the impression that Proust made on Forssgren was even more profound.

Introduction to Forssgren's Memoirs and Related Documents

❖ ❖ ❖

I
T was apparently the publication in 1965 of the second
and concluding volume of George D. Painter's biography
of Marcel Proust—the first major biography of the novelist in English—that provoked Ernest Forssgren to write his
memoirs. He was outraged by Painter's depiction of Proust's
homosexuality and apparently felt that he himself was being
accused as well. Painter himself knew nothing about Forssgren, but the Swede must have told many of his acquaintances in the United States about his service with Proust,
perhaps exaggerating their closeness. The publication of
Painter's biography, the second volume of which provides
many details about Proust's homosexuality, including the
procurement of young men from the servant class—like
Ernest Forssgren—seems to have made him fear for his reputation.

Forssgren left his vitriolic denial of Painter's portrait of
Proust in a typed two-page statement, which he called his

13

"summary" of Painter. He folded this twice and inserted it in his copy of Painter's second volume, which covers the period from December 1903 to Proust's death in 1922. Forssgren also wrote comments in pencil on the relevant pages and on the end pages. He subsequently tried to erase these endpaper comments, but I have been able to reconstruct most of them.

Céleste Albaret revealed Forssgren's given name when she published her memoirs in 1973, but she could not recall his family name. Painter did not have access to Céleste's memoirs or, of course, to a number of others that were published in the wake of his biography. Nor did Painter have most of Proust's correspondence, later published by Philip Kolb in twenty-one volumes. Forssgren wrote his memoirs in 1965, and Céleste published hers in 1973; the excerpts from his appeared in French in 1975. This means that each worked from memory without the benefit—or the disadvantage—of knowing what the other had recorded. As we shall see from their memoirs, each remembered the other vividly, although neither could recall the other's last name.

Forssgren died in 1970, before he could read Céleste's memoirs, which certainly would have infuriated him. Céleste lived until 1984 and the age of ninety-three. If she read and reacted to the excerpts published in French from Forssgren's memoirs, her reaction has not been published. No doubt she would have invalidated much of what he says. Neither memoirist knew the contents of many of Proust's letters from the two periods where Forssgren's and Celeste's accounts coincide—the last trip to Cabourg in 1914 and Proust's final months, August to November 1922. These letters were subsequently annotated and published by Philip Kolb after 1975.

The discovery of the complete, unedited copy of Forssgren's memoirs allows us to compare his and Céleste's recollections with what Proust himself wrote in letters about the

1914 trip to Cabourg. Céleste is the only witness to Proust's death who left recorded testimony of his final days. In matters where Céleste's and Forssgren's recollections vary sharply with Proust's account, it is the writer's letters that become authoritative. Not only are his letters from the source itself, but they also have the advantage of being written at the time—or very nearly so—and, hence, are fresh regarding the events described.

About the Memoirs: "The Mysterious Visit"

The memoirs consist of ninety-three typed pages, double-spaced, produced on a standard typewriter with pica font. Overall, they read like an unedited text whose episodes are told in chronological order. Although Forssgren skips over whole periods of his youth, the adventures he does relate occurred during the ten-year period from 1912 until Proust's death. Since the two main events narrated are the first encounter with Proust in 1914 and the failed Paris rendezvous in 1922, which ends the memoirs, it is clear that it was Forssgren's reaction to Painter's biography that compelled him to tell his story. However, the memoirs contain no mention of Proust's homosexuality or the story about Proust's giving him a copy of Oscar Wilde's *De Profundis* as a kind of test to see how he would react. These interesting revelations are contained in the "summary" of Painter.

We do not know whether Forssgren typed the memoirs himself or wrote them in longhand and then had them typed; perhaps he dictated them to someone who also did the typing. There are only a few instances in which Forssgren did any revising on the typescript; these are all minor, such as the insertion of an inadvertently omitted word or the striking of an inadvertently repeated word. I found only one correction of a typographical error, when "world 'lieutenant'" was typed for "word 'lieutenant.'" Forssgren, or someone, struck through the "l" to make the correction.

In editing the memoirs, I did not correct Forssgren's spelling; many of these errors are probably typographical ones. Often a word misspelled in one place is spelled correctly in another. I have maintained Forssgren's punctuation, except in cases where quotation marks or the closing of parentheses, etc., were unintentionally left out; commas have been added here and there for clarity and readability. These changes have been placed in brackets. All ellipses are Forssgren's own. His capitalization and underscoring are unchanged. For greater ease in reading, I have indented dialogues that he ran together. As for grammar and syntax, I have made changes, enclosed in brackets, only for the sake of clarity. Brief corrections and identifications are given in brackets; lengthier ones and comments are placed in footnotes. I have used the bracketed label *sic* sparingly, only after those mistakes that most suspiciously resemble editorial or typesetting errors.

Regarding Forssgren's French: the memoirs were obviously typed on an American typewriter, which has none of the accent marks necessary for writing in French. Where the French is correct, I have simply added the accent marks and provided a translation. Where the French is incorrect, as is often the case, I correct the error only when confusion seems likely. Similarly, I translate only that French—whether rendered correctly or incorrectly by Forssgren—that is not commonly encountered in English and is not an obvious cognate. We know nothing about Forssgren's circumstances at the time he produced the memoirs. But since he makes some rather large claims about his linguistic abilities and states that French is so clear and logical a language that dictionaries are not even needed when writing in French—in contrast to what he calls the "barbaric" British English pronunciation and spelling—it seems fair to let readers see the memoirs in their original state. And even if Forssgren dictated the document and had someone else do the typing, surely it is reasonable to expect that someone with such linguistic pretensions—as well as the literary ambitions he claimed to have—would have attempted to correct the most obvious errors and inconsistencies.

A small portion of these memoirs was translated and published in French. See "Les Mémoires d'un valet de chambre (Les souvenirs d'Ernest Forssgren)," *Cahiers Marcel Proust,* n.s. 7, *Études proustiennes* 2: 119–42. The memoirs used as the basis of the French version and those now in the Marcel Proust Collection at the Mervyn H. Sterne Library at the University of Alabama at Birmingham are clearly one and the same. As one would expect, the French version omits everything not pertaining to Proust. But surprisingly enough, the French version also leaves out a number of interesting items related to Proust, such as Forssgren's arrival at 102 boulevard Haussmann to apply for a job as a valet, the encounter with Céleste Albaret, whom he took to be Madame Proust, and even the initial interview with Proust himself. According to prefatory remarks by the editors of the French version, Jacques Bersani and Michel Raimond, the translated excerpts from Forssgren's memoirs were brought to one of them by Jean-Pierre Hascoët, who had met Forssgren when Hascoët was a French exchange student at an unspecified university in California. Bersani and Raimond go on to say that it was Hascoët's translation of Forssgren's memoirs, a translation that the memoirs show was faulty in many regards, that they used for their published version, after having "slightly altered it."

A close comparison of the translation to the original memoirs reveals many discrepancies. The only description given by the French editors is that the memoirs in English were about "eighty pages." The actual page count of the photocopy entrusted by Forssgren to Marilyn Gordon is ninety-three. Since the document was typed on a standard American typewriter before the age of computers and their printers, there would have been no variation in the pagination of the original and any photocopies of it. The translator omitted Forssgren's title ("The Mysterious Visit"), the place of composition (San Francisco), and the date (March 2, 1965), all given by Forssgren on his title page. The editors were apparently unaware of the omissions within the segments about Proust and the alterations or mistranslations in the text provided by Hascoët. Furthermore, the editors, in their introduction, attribute to Proust a reaction—not in the original typescript, though they imply it is—to Forssgren's mistaking Céleste for Madame Proust.

The excerpts published in French contain, in addition to some inaccurate translations, the unacknowledged omission of phrases, sentences, and sometimes entire paragraphs. In order not to overburden my annotations, I indicate only the most significant of these discrepancies. Those readers who are bilingual and curious can compare the original memoirs to the excerpts published in the *Cahiers Marcel Proust.*

I remind the reader that none of the information contained in Forssgren's "summary" of Painter's biography—a statement in which he expands on his encounter with Proust—has been published previously. These remarks provide an interesting and at times contradictory supplement to the material contained in the memoirs, as do the remarks that Forssgren scrawled across the pages of his copy of Painter's biography.

At the end of his memoirs, Forssgren adds this caveat: "It is regrettable that I did not keep a diary during the time I was with Monsieur Proust. I am writing this entire account from memory, in retrospect; therefore it is possible it may contain some unintentional inaccuracies and discrepancies." Fair enough. No one would expect him or anyone else to remember with great precision the details of events that had taken place nearly five decades earlier. In my notes and comments, I will provide the factual evidence we have, as well as accounts by other witnesses and by Proust himself.

Here then, for the first time, is the complete text of Forssgren's memoirs.

The Mysterious Visit
by Ernest A. Forssgren

SAN FRANCISCO, MARCH 2, 1965

❖　❖　❖

The Mysterious Visit

❖ ❖ ❖

THIS true story goes back to the beginning of the First World War. I came to Paris with the hope, expectancy and ambition of an optimistic youth of 19 years of age in the year 1913. My goal was to somehow, sometime, eventually be able to enter the great university of Sorbonne for the study of Latin and the Latin languages, principally the French language which I admire and love the most of all languages, for its beauty, refinement, culture and elegance, in which it excels over all other languages. I wanted to become a teacher, a professor of the Romance languages.

Where would I get the money? From my parents I could expect nothing, as they were too poor, and already helping a son through Uppsala University. Indeed, I had to leave school and start out in life on my own, at the age of 13 years, and have been on my own ever since. As a matter of fact I had contributed to my parents, now and then, from my meager earnings as an errand boy, waiter, etc., untill I left Sweden in 1912,

23

never to set foot in that country again, as I then thought. I had been told by an older brother then studying and working in Paris, that, as a domestic servant, "valet de pied[,]" I would get food, room and board as well as clothes plus 100 to 150 francs a month.[1] That would be the best way of saving money, and the work would be easy. As I did not drink or smoke I could save a maximum of money, perhaps as much as 100 francs a month or more. Another advantage: I would have a maximum of leisure time for study and preparation for the University.

Prior to coming to Paris I had spent a few months in London to learn the world language, English, which I had been told was a must. But I soon lost interest in the language where a word was spelled one way and pronounced another. You would require a magical memory in order to remember how to spell a word. Besides, I found it a hidious language, so flat and ugly and so indistinct: fawthah, mothah, brothah.[2] As I had already started to prepare myself for the study of French, I was comparing it with IT, and I asked myself how it was possible that a language so uncouth as spoken by the English could be separated only by a narrow channel from the world's most beautiful language. The only thing that really

1. Henrik Vitalis, archivist of the Church of Sweden, has provided me with documentation indicating that the brother in question was Jonas Alfred Forssgren, the eldest son of Jonas Peter (born 1854) and Karin Kristina Forssgren (born 1864). The archives of the Swedish congregation kept address books; one of these, whose entries begin in 1912, indicates that Alfred Forsgren resided at "47, rue St. Dominique." This address was next door to that of Prince Orloff's Paris mansion and presumably was the service entrance. As we shall see, Forssgren gave the address as 45–47, rue St. Dominique. According to Vitalis, "the rather common name Forssgren is usually spelled Forsgren, and since the pronunciation is the same," it is not surprising to see his name spelled both ways.

2. Forssgren's rendering of the way the English pronounce "father, mother, brother."

stood out as the English was spoken by the "gentry" was arrogance, conceit and affectation, as if they were trying to inject elegance into a language that does not lend itself to IT. What kind of a language is it that a word can be spelled up to ten different ways? No wonder there is all that confusion. How I pity the poor emigrants to America who have to suffer all that, and so NEEDLESSLY. Fortunately, the AMERICAN LANGUAGE is at least a 50% improvement over the English. I decided I never wanted to ever learn English.

Leaving London for Paris was like leaving <u>hell</u> for HEAVEN. How can two cities so close be so different, I asked myself.

I arrived in Paris in the middle of May and loved it right from the start; the people, the language, the beauty, elegance and dignity of the architecture, the charm of the women and their musical speech—I loved everything, the whole of France, its lovely climate as compared with what I had been used to. My stay in France, alas[,] too brief, shall always remain my life's happiest memory.

On my arrival in Paris I had already learned enough from my French lesson-book to get by on. Having obtained the address of the Swedish employment agency on Avenue Mac-Mahon[,] I went there the next day.[3] Together with my older brother, as my spokesman, we were sent to the address of Madame La Marquise de V. adjoining Parc Monceau, and on the strength of my brother's reference and my short one from London, I was engaged to start the next day, 100 francs a month and "all found" except a civilian suit.[4] It was not con-

3. According to the 1912 edition of the *Paris-Hachette,* there was an employment agency (Agence Moderne de Placement) at 7 avenue Mac-Mahon. It seems unlikely that there was an agency devoted entirely to Swedish expatriates.

4. The lovely, elegant Parc de Monceau is located not far from the Arc de Triomphe in the eighth arrondissement, in one of Paris's most fashion-

sidered a good job, but I was in no position to be choosy. I was glad I was able to start earning my living so soon. I figured it would do untill I had a good command of the language. After about a month in Paris we were to leave for the Château de Pontchartrain, the summer palace of the Marquise who was an elderly widow with two spinster daughters.[5] The summer passed quickly as there was a great deal to do, many house guests, and a great deal of entertainments. However, the country was beautiful and I enjoyed roaming in the private park where I spent most of my spare time with my books. I was amazed at myself how rapidly I was improving, but then I was learning a "learnable" language. I was told my accent was "tout à fait parisien" [entirely Parisian], and that was what I wanted most, a native accent.

I was glad when told we were returning to Paris, as I wanted to look for a better job. I had learned, by now, that there was a competition among the wealthy mansions and society salons, vieing for the tallest and handsomest lackeys. Palaces such as Count de Castelane's (Anna Gould's millions), Rothchilds [Rothschilds], Polignac, Périgord, de Ligne, Orloff, etc.[6] I had interviewed some of them but they would

_____

able neighborhoods. Proust and his younger brother, Robert, often played in this park when they were children. "All found" means room, board, and livery provided.

5. The lady in question is the marquise de Villehermose. According to the *Tout-Paris 1913*, she was the proprietor of the château de Pontchartrain, in Seine-et-Oise, now known as Yvelines. In Paris she resided in her mansion at 3 avenue Ruysdaël. Henrik Vitalis says that the first address book of the Swedish Church in Paris contains the notation that Ernest Forssgren lives "chez la marquise de Villehermose at 3 avenue Ruysdaël."

6. Count Boniface de Castellane (1867–1932) married the American heiress Anna Gould (1878–1961). He needed money; she wanted a title. Boni, as he was known, spent a fortune on sumptuous residences and lavish parties that became legendary.

not go higher than 125 francs per month. I figured that if I was being engaged as an ornament, I was ornamental enough to warrant a salary of 150 francs per month and was holding out for it. Only the French will give you credit for anything. It was

---

Count Edmond de Polignac (1834–1901) married Winnaretta Singer (1865–1943), the American heiress to the Singer Sewing Machine fortune. Both were accomplished musicians. In 1865 the prince, at age thirty, won first prize in composition at the Conservatoire National de Musique of Paris. The Polignacs often performed or invited guests to hear professional performers at a studio the prince maintained in the rue Cortambert, where he hired large orchestras and choruses to perform his compositions. Winnaretta, whose mother was French, had been, since the age of sixteen, a friend of Gabriel Fauré's, whom the Polignacs, like Proust, greatly admired. Staunch Wagnerites, the prince and princess were among a number of smart Parisians who made the annual pilgrimage to Bayreuth. Proust evoked their salon, which was devoted to music, in his letters and other writings. See Proust's article on Mme de Polignac's salon, "Le Salon de la Princesse Edmond de Polignac: Musique d'aujourd'hui, échos d'autrefois" (The salon of Princess Edmond de Polignac: Music of today, echoes of days gone by), published in *Le Figaro* in 1903. See *Contre Sainte-Beuve* (Paris: Gallimard, 1971), 465–69. A great patron of the arts, Mme de Polignac endowed the Fondation Singer-Polignac, located in her Paris mansion. Of the wealthy, prominent Parisians mentioned by Forssgren, the only ones closely associated with Proust were Boni de Castellane and the Polignacs. For a recent biography of Mme de Polignac, see Sylvia Kahn, *Music's Modern Muse: A Life of Winnaretta Singer, Princesse de Polignac* (Rochester, N.Y.: University of Rochester Press, 2003).

I am not certain who Périgord is. There is no trace of anyone by this name in Proust's correspondence.

Prince Louis de Ligne, 1854–1918. The same address book mentioned above by Vitalis shows that Forssgren's address was changed from that of the marquise de Villehermose to that of the "Princesse de Vinge," an obvious misreading of Princesse de Ligne, since the princess's correct address is given as "32, rue Babylone." All the Paris names and addresses given by Forssgren are accurate as verified for me by Caroline Szylowicz, Kolb-Proust Librarian at the University of Illinois, who consulted the *Tout-Paris* directory for the years in question.

According to his death certificate, Prince Alexis Orloff (April 6, 1867–

the opinion of many of them, as well as my own, that I was quite a handsome young man, 6'2½" tall with fine teeth and hair, and a charming personality I was told.[7]

Interviewed by Prince Orloff, a descendant of Count Gregory Orloff of Catherine and Peter the Great fame, I was offered 125 francs per month for six months, and after that 150 per month and "all found" plus a civilian suit. I decided to take it as the Prince was a bachelor and away a great deal, giving me plenty of leisure to study. I figured if I held on to such a job for two years I would save enough for enrollment in the University, and plenty of time to prepare myself for it. As I had hoped, the position at Prince Orloff's turned out rather well. We were four men in livery and would alternate every other day on duty in the antechamber, 2 and 2 were free every other day from noon untill 6 o'clock and every other Sunday

---

October 2, 1916) was attaché to the Imperial Russian Embassy in Paris. In addition to his Paris mansion at 45 rue Saint-Dominique, the prince owned the château de Bellefontaine (Seine-et-Marne). At the outbreak of the war, the prince was already suffering from the illness that killed him two years later. Céleste Albaret relates this anecdote: "Albert [Le Cuziat] had told M. Proust a story" about Count [Prince] Orloff "which both amused and shocked him. Right in the middle of a big dinner-party, the count sent for his chamber pot and relieved himself in front of the guests. 'Worse than the royal close-stool of the old days,' said M. Proust." Céleste Albaret, *Monsieur Proust,* as told to Georges Belmont, trans. Barbara Bray (New York: New York Review of Books, 2003), 192. There is no direct mention of Prince Orloff in any of Proust's known letters. The correct title is prince and not count, which Céleste may have gotten from George D. Painter's biography of Proust. As we shall see, Forssgren corrected the error in his own copy of Painter.

7. In a letter to Mme de Clermont-Tonnerre, Proust recalled that Forssgren was strikingly handsome. See *SL* 4: 181 n. 1. Céleste writes that she and Proust used to joke about Forssgren's conceit. According to her he was "as pleased with himself as if he were the King of Sweden, if not God Almighty." Albaret, *Monsieur Proust,* 29.

free all day. (The entire staff consisted of some 30 servants.) This gave me plenty of time for study, and I could study even on duty in the antechamber. I was always with my books and came to be regarded as a book worm.[8] My colleagues would chide me, telling me not to stay too long in my subjunctive mood, referring to grammatical terms I would sometimes discuss with them. Our duty in the antechamber was to receive guests and be handy for anything the Prince or guests might want, and to serve meals in a very elaborate dining room.

The prince was not hard to work for, but probably due to his many ailments he was rather cranky and quick of temper, but on the whole essentially fair. To illustrate I shall mention an incident, rather dramatic and amusing, that took place one evening when the Prince came back from the opera with Mademoiselle de S., his favorite mistress.[9] It was near 12 o'clock. I had dozed off and did not hear the first light tap on the horn of his very elegant and luxurious Rolls-Royce.[10] It was the footman's duty to help him out of the car, as he had

8. Forssgren admits, in his "Summary" of Painter, that he never read Proust.

9. Cornelia Otis Skinner, in her delightful book *Elegant Wits and Grand Horizontals* ([Boston: Houghton Mifflin, 1962], 226), confirms Orloff's reputation as a womanizer. According to her, Prince Orloff came to Paris after losing "his position in the Tsar's army" as the result of a quarrel and subsequent duel with a German officer. The nature of the duel was unusual: a contest to see who could down the most liqueur glasses of Cointreau. The German passed out after the eightieth round, but Orloff kept on going until he had swallowed "one hundred and twelve glassfuls, then rose and walked away seemingly fresh as a daisy." The following day, however, the cocky victor nearly died from a liver attack. The tsar exiled the reckless Orloff to Paris "in the not too harsh severity of a palace on the rue Saint-Dominique, a château near Fontainebleau, the position of secretary to the Russian embassy and an uninterrupted series of love affairs."

10. The phrase "elegant and luxurious" was changed by hand—whether Forssgren's is unclear—to "elegant, luxurious."

difficulty of movement and always walked with a cane. He had waited perhaps one minute untill the second honk woke me up, and I rushed out to open the car door only to be greeted with a long string of names and abusive epithets all the way in to the antechamber. Well, I had quite a temper of my own and shouted back at him, "You can't call me names like that!" and let out a string of some choice epithets in Swedish, as I threw the large, genuine Russian sable car robe over him, and almost burst out laughing at the comical scene, he trying to shed the robe poking with his free hand untill it finally dropped to the floor. I quickly picked it up as the Prince stood staring at me for a few seconds in disbelief, and Mlle de S, pale as a ghost, obviously expecting to witness a murder, not knowing which of us would end up the murderer. He came toward me lifting his cane to strike me. I just stood there throwing my chest out, and shouting to him in Swedish: "I dare you to strike me, for it will be your last act."[11]

What he read in my face caused him to hesitate. He slowly lowered his cane, muttering, "Méfiez-vous, ça ne prendra pas" [Be careful, that won't do][,] as he stalked into the elevator, which I had just opened for him, ahead of Mademoiselle who gave me a rather enigmatic smile, as I closed the door on her. I thought of all the times she had smiled so charmingly at me, which had sent my mind awondering. . . . I had called the Prince's bluff and he had called mine, so we were even. Of course, I would not have hurt him, but I am not so sure if he might not have struck me with the cane if he had thought he would have gotten away with it.

I realized, much to my regret, I had lost my job, my own doing. I could have curbed my temper, but was I going to take all those insults? Wasn't it understandable I might have

11. The word "for" was deleted by the same unknown hand.

dozed off for a few minutes that time of night; hadn't I some self-respect? I had acted quite right; I was as good as he and a whole lot better I told myself. I had acted just right. I could easily get another job. Having sneaked some books from the Prince's library on Russian history in general and the Orloff history in particular, I had found the princely title rather ill-gotten. Count Orloff, one of Catherine's favorites, had been raised to prinedom [sic] for certain services rendered. There was some intrigue having to do with the untimely demise of Tsar Peter.[12] These things had vaguely entered my mind as I tried to find excuses to justify my incredible action. Certainly no servant in all of Paris would have dared to do what I did. However, I had no fear of the guilotine, but I was worried about not getting a good reference, and I had already been in the service of the Prince close to a year.

Getting to my room I found it impossible to sleep and started packing for departure the next day, realizing I would not be tolerated in the house another day after having committed what almost amounted to "lèse majestée". In the morning I went down to the servant's dining hall for my petit dé-jeuner. Everything was as usual. There probably won't be any action untill lunchtime, as the Prince always slept late. I went about my duties as if nothing had happened. I had just had my lunch and as I was leaving the dining room I met Monsieur Pralon, the secrétaire, coming from the Prince's apartment.[13]

12. A reference to Orloff's presumed ancestors, the brothers Grigorii and Aleksei Orlov. Grigorii was Catherine's lover. She gave birth to his son on April 11, 1762, less than three months before the murder of Peter III on June 28. Aleksei took full responsibility for the assassination in a letter not made public until 1881. See John T. Alexander, *Catherine the Great: Life and Legend* (New York: Oxford University Press, 1898), 3–4, 15, 60.

13. Among the witnesses who signed the prince's death certificate was Alexandre Pralon, who described himself as Orloff's secretary.

Ah, here falls the axe I thought, but, to my amazement, he passed me with his usual affable "bon Jour Ernest." I didn't know what to make of things. I went to my room to put on my livery for my turn in the antechamber. We were having a large dinner party and I had to forego my usual day off.

I was sitting on the sofa in the antechamber, having pulled out the drawer of the elegant Louis 16th writing table where I kept my study books, and was in the midst of my study when I heard a voice calling, "Airnest, Air-nest! Venez-ici" [Come here]. It was the Prince calling from the top of his royal stairway. What now, I wondered? He always used the elevator. "Today I am climbing the stairs, please come and help me down, I need the exercise[,] don't you think?" I quickly ascended the stairs and turned around as the prince indicated he wanted to lean on my shoulders as we descended. Never in my life had I expected a situation like this. He said in very conciliatory tones, "Ernest, are you still angry with me?"

"Of course not, Prince," I blurted out as if I was talking to a fellow servant.

He burst out laughing like I had never heard him before, "Airnest, I want to tell you something but in the strictest confidence, you understand. Of all my servants in my house, you and Maxime are the only ones I have the greatest respect for. I know I can depend on you and where I have you, and I appreciate it no end. The other cowering, fawning, creeping creatures I have no respect for at all. From the first of the month you shall have 25 francs raise in salary. I have given M. Pralon orders."

I was the happiest man imaginable.

But, alas, all good things must come to an end eventually, like all bad things. The gathering war clouds started darkening, and finally the war was declared on the 2nd of August,

1914.[14] I shall pass up describing the confusion and chaos that so suddenly overwhelmed Paris, leaving it to the reader's imagination. That terrific drive toward Paris, the indescribable slaughter, the terrible cataclysm. . . . The Kaiser had expected to take Paris by the end of August and planned to celebrate with a gala dinner at the Café de Paris. Newspaper headlines warned people, able to do so, to leave Paris.

The Prince ordered his Mansion closed and most of the servants to be dismissed on their own for the duration of the war or untill such time as Paris would be inhabitable again, in which case all would be welcome back. He was leaving for his villa in Pau, in the Basque country[,] and was only taking his most important staff members, as the villa could only accommodate ten or twelve employees and there was the war going on.[15] Now I was faced with the problem of what to do. I scanned the newspaper and found an ad asking for a valet de chambre to leave Paris with a semi-invalid gentleman. S'adresser [s'adresser: inquire at] 88 Boulevard Haussmann, Proust.[16]

14. On August 2, 1914, the French government ordered the mobilization of the army; Germany declared war on France on August 3.

15. Pau is a city in southwestern France where a number of prominent Parisians sought refuge after the outbreak of the war. Among those close to Proust who went there were Mme Geneviève Straus and Marthe Proust, wife of Dr. Robert Proust, with their ten-year-old daughter Adrienne-Suzanne. Robert Proust was mobilized on the first day of the war and sent to the front at Verdun, where he immediately began to operate on wounded soldiers.

16. The correct address is, of course, 102 boulevard Haussmann, where Proust lived from late 1906 until 1919 and where he wrote most of *In Search of Lost Time*. His famous cork-lined room was re-created with some of the original furniture and memorabilia in the documentary film, *Marcel Proust: A Writer's Life*, 1993. Visitors to Paris can see two re-creations of the bed-

The lady that answered the door was a rather pale and tired looking person, but otherwise of obvious culture and refinement. I took her to be Madame Proust.[17] She explained that Monsieur Proust, as a semi-invalid, spent most of his time in bed, writing, and to please excuse the appearance of the room. She ushered me into a most depressing room, windows covered with woolen blankets to keep out damp air and light, it was explained later. There was a peculiar odor of some burning vegetation, which was explained to me to be the result of burning a green powder to aleviate the asthma of which M[.] Proust suffered. The only lighting consisted of two candles casting a spectral shadow over the whole room as well as [over] his rather cadaverous-appearing face, although it had an aura of a christlike kindliness.[18] The eyes were his most striking features, large and dark with almost luminous shining whites. I told him about my position with Prince Orloff and that I had been in his employ about a year. The Prince's house had been closed and most of the servants laid

---

room. One is at the Musée Carnavalet in Paris and the other is at 102 boulevard Haussmann, where the Varin-Bernier Bank, which purchased the building in 1919, has recently restored it. For a long time the room served as the office of the bank's president, who, after years of requests by Proust's admirers to see it, gracefully and generously relocated his office to another room.

17. According to Céleste, Forssgren was at least the second person interviewed for this post. Her memory is confirmed by Proust's correspondence. See SL 3: 276. She recalled that the first young man interviewed took her for Madame Proust. Did he and Forssgren both make the same mistake or did she attribute Forssgren's impression to the first applicant? Albaret, *Monsieur Proust*, 28.

18. The light that Forssgren saw was probably from Proust's bedside lamp. Proust did not burn candles next to his bed, but a candle was kept lit in the corridor during the night (that is, the day) in case he had an urgent need to light his asthma powder. See Albaret, *Monsieur Proust*, 16, 325.

off, but were expected back at the end of the war or until such time as he would be able to return to Paris. He could check with the secretary of the Prince[,] who was still in Paris[,] for a reference. He asked my nationality and I told him Swedish.

"Pas possible, vous parles tout à fait comme un parisien"— you speak like a Parisian, you must have talent for languages.[19]

"It is strange you should mention that, Monsieur. I came to Paris with the one great object of my life, namely to study to become a professor in the Latin languages, specializing in French, and when you love a language like I love yours, you strive for perfection."

"Quel charmant compliment, Monsieur Ernest! Vous y irez loin, j'en suis sure."[20]

"I hope some day to be able to enroll in your great university, of Sorbonne, Monsieur."

"When can you come and work for me?"

"Aren't you going to check my reference before you decide, Monsieur?"

"I have already checked. Your speech, manner and appearance are your best reference, but I will check with M. Pralon later. You are a remarkable young man." I gave [him] the phone number to the Prince's secretariat.

"I shall ring for Céleste, ma cuisinière [my cook], who will show you your room, which will be only for a day or so.[21] We

19. Aside from the incorrect ending for *parlez,* Forssgren had rendered the French correctly here. He has provided a partial translation. *Pas possible* means impossible.

20. "What a charming compliment, Monsieur Ernest!" Vous irez loin, j'en suis sûr: You will go far, I'm sure.

21. According to Céleste's own testimony, she knew virtually nothing about cooking and running a household when she assumed her post as Proust's housekeeper on a permanent basis, about two weeks before Forssgren came for the interview. In her memoirs, she tells an amusing anecdote about Proust's first culinary request; he asked for fried eggs and she pre-

will leave for Cabourg as soon as we can be ready. Are you satisfied with 125 francs a month to start?"

"I am satisfied," I said. "The lady who presented me, is she your housekeeper?"

"Yes, she is the wife of my chauffeur valet de chambre who has been called to the colors, a very fine man, this terrible war!"[22]

"This Madame d'Alvarez [Albaret] strikes me as a lady of quality. On dirait une véritable dame du mond."[23]

"You are a very observant young man. A statement like that would ordinarily come from an homme du monde [man of the world]. I think we shall get along well."

"I took the lady to be Madame Proust."

"Non, je suis célibataire." [No, I am single.]

"It is very interesting to learn that you are a writer, Monsieur. I myself have ambition in that direction. It goes with the study of languages, some day, maybe. . . ."

"Do you type?" M[.] Proust asked. "My publisher would prefer my manuscripts typed as they have difficulty with my handwriting. It is rather illegible."[24]

"I have always wanted to learn to type and I expect to do so at the earliest opportunity," I said.[25]

---

pared scrambled ones because she did not know the difference. See Albaret, *Monsieur Proust*, 75.

See the "Summary," where Forssgren says he came to 102 boulevard Haussmann on the day of the trip to Cabourg.

22. Odilon Albaret was Proust's driver. Nicolas Cottin served as the novelist's valet until the beginning of the war, which he did not survive.

23. One would say she is a real society lady. Forssgren misspells *monde*.

24. Proust wrote his vast novel in bed at night; his handwriting is notoriously difficult to read.

25. It is clear from documents that Forssgren wrote many years later in the United States that he eventually did learn to type.

"Would you be interested [in] typing my manuscripts?"

"I would be most delighted. It would be in line with my studies." I began to think this was what I was really looking for. I could work for M[.] Proust and study at the University at the same time. This kindly gentleman would let me arrange things.[26]

Since Monsieur Proust's initials are M.P. (for Marcel Proust) I wish to state here that the abbreviation MP stands for Monsieur Proust.[27] At no time did I ever address him in any other way. MC designates Madame Céleste (d'Alvarez) [Céleste Albaret] as a semi-formal address of the "fellow" employee for whom I had great respect and admiration.[28]

It had been announced in the papers that people leaving Paris by train would only be allowed to take handbaggage.[29] I was allowed to leave most of my things at Prince Orloff's and arrived at MP's apartment with only one valise containing the most essential things for my needs.[30] I told MP about hand-

26. There is no evidence that Forssgren ever typed or took dictation for Proust.

27. As we shall see, Forssgren does not use these abbreviations consistently.

28. The feeling was not mutual, as we have seen. Forssgren's inability to give Proust's correct street address and Céleste's correct surname may be taken as proof that he did not read his copy of Painter's biography thoroughly and carefully. Forssgren describes his cursory reading of the biography in his "Summary."

29. The excerpts published in French (*Cahiers Marcel Proust*, n.s. 7, *Études proustiennes* 2: 119–42) begin with this sentence. See my introduction, pages 17–18.

30. Forssgren provides additional details about his circumstances at the time in his "Summary," where he also gives a slightly different time scheme: "When I answered his ad as I describe in my story, I had never heard of M.P. and did not know any more of him than he about me. I did not stay in his apartment in Paris until we came back from Cabourg. I went direct[ly] from Prince Orloff to his apartment and then to the train the same day."

baggage only. I was sent to the Gare du Nord to buy tickets for three, first class, for the next day.[31] MP had telegraphed ahead engaging a suite of three rooms at the Grand Hotel de Cabourg, a bathing resort on the Normandie coast. We left the apartment in plenty of time for the scheduled train departure, carrying our baggage, I carrying two valises and MC carrying her own.[32] There were no taxis available, having been requisitioned by the war department. We were appalled to find that our accommodations were taken and the whole coach packed with people like sardines.[33] No one could get in or out. I tried to find an official for explanation regarding our accommodations. The functionaire [fonctionnaire: official] I finally reached told me there was nothing anyone could do. It was a case of first come, first served and everyone for himself. It seemed as if all the coaches were filled already. People were everywhere. We began to despair of ever getting out of Paris except by walking. Towards the rear of the train I found a coach (fourth class, there were four classes those days) that looked like we might be able to squeeze into. Showing our tickets and pleading [the] invalidism of MP we

31. Forssgren has apparently forgotten that the Paris railway station serving Cabourg was the Gare Saint-Lazare.

32. Céleste's version of this last trip to Cabourg—in her case the first as well—differs on several points from Forssgren's. According to her, Proust had two pieces of luggage, one a large suitcase that he used for his manuscripts and that he always kept with him, the other a huge trunk with wheels, into which he put everything else, clothes, his linen and bedclothes, sweaters, two coats, and all the medicines to treat his asthma and other ailments. Céleste packed these bags under Proust's supervision. The luggage to be checked was turned over to the boulevard Haussmann concierge Antoine Bertholhomme, who called the railway company to send a truck to pick it up. The valise with the manuscripts remained with Proust. Albaret, *Monsieur Proust,* 29–30. Presumably, Forssgren was carrying his own valise and the one containing the manuscripts.

33. The train had been requisitioned by the military.

managed finally to get into the coach after much bosculat-ing.[34] An elderly man got up and relinquished his seat to MP. I managed to bring along the two valises by holding them overhead, and MC had to do the same with hers. It took all my strength to accomplish it. We were able to place our bag-gage in racks above. Madame Céleste and I would, of course, have to stand the entire journey. MP was so cramped that I began to doubt he was going to make it. We were so packed that there wasn't a person who did not touch another in every direction. It seemed like hours before the train finally started to move. It was carrying people even on the roofs of all the coaches. We heard rumors the engine was having difficulty getting up enough steam to haul the enormous load. It was moving so slowly that I could have walked as fast. Indeed I would have preferred it but there was no way of getting out. It is impossible to describe the torturous ordeal we had to en-dure for 13 to 14 hours without food or drink, until we finally reached Mézidon where we were to change trains.[35] To have

34. The erstwhile linguist has created a new word by anglicizing "bous-culer," French for pushing and shoving.

35. Mézidon is a town in the canton of Calvados. On Monday, Septem-ber 7, 1914, just a few days after the group arrived in Cabourg, Proust wrote a letter on hotel stationery to Mme Catusse, a close friend, to whom he de-scribed the trip, saying that the night was spent on the train: "I left for my usual Cabourg, which is four hours from Paris. But the train took twenty-two hours and was so crowded that one couldn't even sit down." SL 3: 277. Forssgren's recollection, overall, seems more accurate than that of Céleste, who depicts the trip as fairly uneventful, although she, like Proust, said it took "infinitely longer" than usual. According to her, she rode with Proust in one compartment and Forssgren rode in the next. Albaret, *Monsieur Proust,* 47. Forssgren's account is more dramatic, even life-threatening for Proust. Proust's letters contain no indication that he suffered unduly from the ex-perience. Had they endured all that Forssgren claims and been obliged to stay overnight in Mézidon, surely Proust would have mentioned the ordeal in the letter to Mme Catusse.

gone on to Cabourg on the same train would probably have meant death for MP. Fortunately MC had very providently brought along a thermos bottle of hot milk for MP, otherwise the outcome for him might have been doubtful. The relief to get off the train was indescribable. MP was half dead and I had to carry him, but he revived quickly as soon as we got outside.[36] Two babies had died in our coach—what misery! Some British soldiers got up and relinquished their seats in the waiting room when they saw our condition. There was a contingent of British soldiers who were waiting for a train to take them to the front. Some of the tracks had been blown up by the enemy so they had to wait until the tracks were restored.

I excused myself to MP and MC, explaining I would go to the local hotel nearby and arrange for accommodations for them. After rousing the sleeping proprietor I was glad to find there was room available and engaged two for MP and MC. I also asked if he could arrange for some food after explaining about our horrendous journey from Paris. He was very sympathetic and promised he would do what he could. As for myself I figured I could manage somehow at the station, as I was anxious to find out about train accommodation for Cabourg. I returned to the station and told MP I had engaged rooms for him and MC. As for myself I had to busy myself regarding the continuation of our journey. I also told them the hotel proprietor would arrange something to eat and drink. After MC had retrieved some toilet articles from the valises, we checked them at the station. I walked with them to the hotel where we were welcomed with some delicious edibles, and it did not take long for us to begin to feel normal again after a hasty clean-up in our respective rooms. After being satisfied that

36. This statement is very suspect.

MP and MC would be comfortable, I returned to the station and asked the lone attendant if there was any news about the next train for Cabourg, but was told that there was nothing yet. I told him I would be resting in the waiting room and to let me know as soon as he had some news. It was now about 4 AM. I found a bench that had shortly before been occupied by some soldiers who were now stretching themselves outside. I laid down and fell asleep right away.

After about four hours of fitful sleep on the hard wooden bench I woke up quite refreshed. I walked back to the hotel where I found the proprietor up and about and asked him about my "wards." They were evidently sleeping comfortably, as he had not heard from them. I washed up and went to find a restaurant and enjoyed my petit déjeuner consisting of café au lait and croissants. I walked back to the gare and began to fraternize with the British soldiers, giving myself a chance to exercise my neglected, limited English. They had been there since the previous day and did not know when they would continue to the front. It depended on how soon the bomb-damaged railroad track would be restored—maybe anytime now.

The young man I was talking to asked for a cigarette, but I had to tell him I did not have any since I did not smoke. The soldiers had already bought up all the tobacco available, and there was no more to be had. As I have always been a problem solver, it is sort of a mania with me, I told him I would try and do something about it. Although I did not smoke, I realized what it might mean to those soldiers to go without tobacco, especially under the circumstances. As I looked at that group of fine, strong and healthy young men, headed for slaughter, I was seized with an overwhelming feeling of pity—the futility, the incredible folly of war. The fatalistic young man I was talking to said, "You know, in a few days our carcasses will be strewn all over, rotting, stinking on the field of 'honor'.

'Honor' they call it; to me it is nothing but bloody 'ell." (There seemed to be a shortage of everything everywhere.)

True to my promise, I looked around for a bicycle to rent, as I knew it would be the only means of transportation which might be available. I found a bicycle shop where I could rent one for 5 francs an hour. I had to put up 100 francs for security, and voilà my transportation to the nearest small town whose name has slipped my mind. I thought of telephoning to find out about availability of tobacco, but I decided I wanted to make the jaunt into the country anyway. I stopped by the hotel and left [a] message that if MP should wake up to tell him that there will not be a train for Cabourg before 4 o'clock in the afternoon, and to say that I decided to take a bicycle tour in the country, and would be back in two or three hours. I was on my way, enjoying the lovely countryside and arriving at a small town after about an hour and a half.[37] I was glad to find that there was a limited amount of tobacco to be had. There were cigarettes and tobacco for pipes and for rolling, but I was allowed only 100 francs worth, which I managed to carry attached to the handle bars, and headed back for Mézidon, joyfully. You can imagine the wonderful reception I got from the soldiers as I handed over all the tobacco. It was great! I had suddenly become a hero and enjoyed the adulation fully. They offered to pay for the tobacco, but I told them it would completely spoil my pleasure and I wouldn't hear of it. I told them I was leaving for Cabourg on the 4 o'clock train with the lady and gentleman that they had showed kindness to earlier in the morning.

It was train time, and we had all had lunch. MP had recovered remarkably and MC looked fine. We walked slowly to the station and noticed we would have a ten minute wait if

37. Forssgren typed "about and hour and a half."

the train was on schedule. A bunch of soldiers were looking in our direction now and then. After a few minutes a delegation of eight or ten soldiers came up to us saluting very smartly. They started to shake hands with me, thanking me for my friendly "tobacco gesture," wishing me good luck, good health and bon voyage, bowing very respectfully at MP and MC as they left.

"What is this?" MP asked. "One would think you were some great hero, this display of cordiality."

"In a very small way your assumption is true, but let us say it is the result of fraternity," I said, smiling impishly. Suddenly a soldier who spoke some French came up and "spilled the beans" even saying I had refused payment for the tobacco.

"Ah," [Monsieur Proust said,] "your bicycle tour in the country for fresh air. I shall have something to say about this when we get to Cabourg. Here comes our train."

We were ready, having redeemed our baggage and happy to note the train was not overloaded with passengers. Off we were with the whole soldier contingent waving at us. In about two hours we would be in Cabourg.

Arriving at the hotel I was pleasantly surprised at our wonderful accommodations. A suite of three rooms with bathroom facilities for each.[38] MP's room already had the windows lined with heavy blankets hidden with beautiful filigree curtains. MP ordered meals to be served in our separate rooms. The first two floors had been converted into an auxiliary hospital for wounded soldiers, and thus the regular guest dining rooms were utilized. I could see that there was not going to be much for me to do, so I asked MP if I could volunteer my services, as such, to the hospital.

38. Forssgren's description of the accommodations matches that of Céleste. See Albaret, *Monsieur Proust*, 30–31.

"You would think of that so soon. It is wonderful of you to want to do so. Of course you can. You are a very fine young man." MP seemed deeply touched.

"I must confess it is partly selfishness on my part as you are not going to have enough for me to do, and I can't stand idleness. Besides I am sure my help is needed in the hospital."

The next morning, after a wonderful sleep, I was up, dressed and ready when MP called for me.

"About the money you spent for the soldiers, how much was it?"

"One hundred francs, that was all they would let me buy."

"Here, this will reimburse you and reward you for your thoughtfulness and resourcefulness."

He tried to hand me a 500 franc note, then worth $100.

"I cannot take it," I said.

"Why, anyone else would under the circumstances; why are you any different? I am a rich man and it means nothing to me, but it would help you toward the realization of your ambition to study."

"Mon cher Monsieur I would like to, but I cannot break a sacred promise I have made to my beloved father and my mother."

"Tell me about your parents."

"I shall love to. My parents are integrity personified. My father taught me that accepting money or material consideration for something I had never earned would eventually lead to disaster. It would lead to covetousness and greed, man's worst vices. 'Promise, my son, that you will never be guilty of this sin.' I promised enthusiastically. The crime of lying is the worst of all crimes. But for lies no war could ever be possible. 'Promise, my son, always adhere to truth.' I promised. So there you see I cannot accept money I have not earned honestly. I promised my mother I would never smoke or drink, and so far I have kept that promise.[39] If I may be so bold as to say so, I have received from my parents an inheritance worth far more than money. I have received good character, good physique, good health and some good looks. Some day I would like to show you the pictures of my parents and you will agree that they are an extraordinary handsome pair and, with integrity to go with it, they are, indeed, a rare combination. So you see why I cannot break my vow. Let us once and for all have this understanding: never tempt me with any money I have never earned, for I cannot accept it. As for the measly 100 francs, what is that compared to these boys giving up their lives?"

"What an extraordinary young man you are!"

It was suggested by the head matron of the hospital, a Countess de M., who happened to be a friend of MP, that I work mornings from 8 to 12.[40] Four hours would be sufficient, since I had my regular work to do.

"It is kind of MP to let you do this, and also kind of you to want to do it."

This arrangement would suit both MP and myself. The hotel was nearly filled and most of the lady guests as well as some of the men were volunteering to work. C'est la guerre. Soon things [became] routine. I was to be sort of a male nurse. It was heartbreaking to see the sufferings of the wounded who were remarkably brave and patient. Most of

---

39. In his later years in America, Forssgren became a heavy drinker. Those who knew him recall, that although he never appeared to be drunk, he liked to start drinking manhattans or gin and tonics at lunch and again before dinner.

40. There is a letter in which Proust refers to a "Comtesse de M." Philip Kolb speculates that she might be the comtesse de Maleville, about whom little is known. Corr. 12: xxii.

them were helpless and had to be handled like babies. It took me a while to get used to the work. I was thinking how lucky I was, not to be one of the victims.[41]

After my hospital work I would take a dip in the ocean and then have my lunch in the hotel staff's dining room where MC would also have her meals. MP, who was on a very strict,

41. Forssgren and Céleste differ here; she apparently forgot about the wounded at Cabourg: "As a matter of fact, we never saw one right up to the last day. I know that people said otherwise later—that M. Proust used to go to see the wounded soldiers, and even that he spent so much money buying them cigarettes and candies that he soon had none left and had to go home. All invention." She does, however, say that the scarcity of cash, due to the wartime suspension of normal banking operations, was a major factor in Proust's decision to leave Cabourg. Proust's money evaporated, she says, on lavish spending for the rooms and tips. Albaret, *Monsieur Proust*, 35–36. Proust's letters written at the time show that Céleste's recollection is faulty. Forssgren, on the other hand, is apparently exaggerating the severity of the wounds, presumably to heighten the drama. In a letter written from Cabourg, Proust says that there were "hundreds of wounded here" but that nearly all of them were all right, "not being gravely wounded, eating, sleeping, walking about." *Corr.* 13: 303. Clearly, the more seriously wounded soldiers were not being sent as far away from the front as Cabourg for treatment and convalescence. In two letters Proust describes the daily gifts he took to the soldiers, usually playing cards, games like checkers, and cigarettes. He makes no mention of Forssgren doing the same with his own money and then being discovered by Proust as the soldiers' benefactor. Proust's version is the most credible. Céleste describes him as being up and about often at Cabourg, and he must have been curious to meet and talk to the soldiers to glean information about the war. Albaret, *Monsieur Proust*, 32. He also wanted to do whatever he could to cheer them up. See *Corr.* 13: 303, 354. In a letter written in early 1915 to Reynaldo Hahn's sister Mme de Madrazo, Proust writes: "At Cabourg . . . one day when I brought some draught sets to the black soldiers (Senegalese and Moroccans) who are fond of that game, a very stupid lady (there seem to be a particularly large number of them at Cabourg) came to stare at them as though they were quaint animals and said to one of them: 'Good morning nigger' which offended him horribly. 'Me nigger,' he retorted, 'you old cow.' When I brought the wounded a few dozen packs of playing-cards they complained that they

light diet, would be served in his room, supervised by MC.[42] His room would be aired, cleaned and [the] bed made by MC about 10 o'clock every morning. While this took about an hour he would rest in my room, since I was working in the hospital. I would take care of my own room as the hotel was short of help.

It was convenient and expedient for MP to have me read the war news to him, as well as book reading, for about an hour every day. He liked it as it was restful to him. An expert in the French language as he was, I could hardly expect a better teacher.[43] He would correct my pronunciation now and again, and seemed to delight in teaching me the language, and I was most appreciative. I was learning French and was paid for it. He was fond of playing checkers, which we played almost every day, alternating with card playing or chess sometimes.[44] Chess he found too taxing on the brain, to which I

---

weren't poker sets (with jokers if that's the right word). I returned with the packs in question, and then they complained that they couldn't play bridge." *SL* 3: 297. Proust used this incident in *Within a Budding Grove* (2: 148–49), where the offending remark is attributed to Mme Blatin.

42. Proust continued to eat relatively little. In any case, Céleste served him only coffee, and he did not remain in his room to eat; he usually came down to the lobby and restaurant area in the evening around dinnertime but did not dine. See Albaret, *Monsieur Proust,* 31.

43. The translation is not accurate here: "Il eût pu, assurément, souhaiter un meilleur lecteur": He [Proust] could certainly have hoped for a better reader.

44. René Gimpel, an art dealer, who knew Proust at Cabourg, remembered that from the time of his first stay, the writer used to go back up to his room around midnight and play checkers with one of the servants whom he interrogated about everything that was happening in the hotel. This practice allowed Proust to amuse himself in the company of attractive young men while collecting material for his novel. See Gimpel, *Diary of an Art Dealer,* trans. John Rosenberg, (New York: Universe, 1987), 174.

agreed. I taught him some card games and did some card tricks I had learned from my father who was an expert amateur magician. These tricks would amaze him although they were quite simple. It developed that my principal job was to keep him from being bored.[45] I was some sort of royal jester, so to speak. He did not seem to be in the mood for much writing. The war news had much to do with that. He had become listless and restive. The weather was rather damp and rainy most of the time, and he could not venture out except when it was sunny and dry.[46]

The war trend had shifted. The blitz drive the Kaiser had

45. Here Céleste agrees: "M. Proust hardly ever made any demands on him." Yet according to her, Forssgren failed even at the little he was asked to do. Proust told her that Forssgren's behavior "gets on my nerves." Albaret, *Monsieur Proust*, 33. For these reasons, Proust told her on their return to Paris that he did not want to keep Forssgren as his valet, nor did he want to try to find another replacement, given the scarcity of young men. He asked whether she felt comfortable staying on, and she agreed to do so. She ran his household until his death, eight years later. Albaret, *Monsieur Proust*, 37–38. For a discussion of the practice of hiring handsome footmen for sex and the indelible impression that Forssgren's good looks made on Proust, see William C. Carter, *Proust in Love* (New Haven: Yale University Press, 2006), chapter 10.

46. The translator has altered this to: "Aussi M. P. ne s'aventurait-il que très exceptionnellement au dehors": And so M. Proust rarely went outdoors. The rainy weather and Proust's inactivity do not fit with Céleste's account. We see that Forssgren and Proust agree about the presence of wounded soldiers but that Forssgren claims it was he who went to visit them and bring them presents and suggests that Proust was too ill or too confined to do so. Céleste's and Proust's accounts match, not regarding the presence of the soldiers but in describing him as being much more active. At Cabourg, as compared with Paris, he was up and about more during the daytime hours and often walked on the promenade that runs in front of the hotel along the shore, today known as the Promenade Marcel Proust. He also visited the soldiers. The passive, semi-invalid Proust, resting in his room or in Forssgren's while his own was being cleaned, seems to be an invention of Forssgren's. See Albaret, *Monsieur Proust*, 37, 34–35.

counted on to take Paris by the end of August had failed. The Germans were halted some 20 kilometers north northeast of Paris by the combined British and French forces. The lines were held and the Germans repulsed here and there. Optimism was reigning and it was thought that the Germans would never take Paris. The war was evolving into a world war. All kinds of rumors were spreading. The Scandinavian countries and Holland would be drawn in. The Kaiser's submarines were playing havoc with the world shipping, causing speculation as to what America might do. Sweden had declared neutrality, but rumors persisted that she would enter the halocaust on the side of Germany. Sweden had enjoyed peace for over 100 years, but for a small country she had become a mighty power to be reckoned with. It was rumored that the Queen, a cousin of the Kaiser, was exerting every effort to get Sweden to join the war on the side of Germany. It seemed that the war was going to be a long, drawn-out affair.

Time went on. Word came that it would be safe to return to Paris. I don't recall how long we had stayed in Cabourg. It was now probably close to Christmas.[47] MP announced we would return to Paris in a week. Shortly before we left Cabourg there arrived to the hospital a very seriously wounded soldier who required an operation that only one doctor could

47. Forssgren's memory is faulty here. According to the chronology established by Philip Kolb based on evidence in Proust's letters and on external sources, the Cabourg stay was from September 3 to October 13 or 14. See *Corr.* 13: 15. Céleste also remembered the vacation as being relatively short. And, in any case, the Grand-Hôtel was open only during the summer months. Proust normally left before October. Céleste says that on this last trip, he obtained permission as a "special favor" to stay after most of the other guests had left. She says they returned to Paris near the end of September. If Proust did remain in the hotel until October 14, as Kolb believes, this must have been due to the staff's indulgence. See Albaret, *Monsieur Proust*, 35.

perform, a famous surgeon, Dr. Chambon, head of the general hospital in Caen, 33 kilometers southwest of Cabourg.[48] The doctor could not be reached by telephone nor telegraph as enemy spies had cut communication facilities. A doctor asked for a volunteer to take a message to Dr. Chambon. Thinking of my bicycle venture in Mézidon, I offered to go, explaining that the only means of transportation would be by bicycle. The doctor knew this and said it was the best we could do under the circumstances. He scribbled a note and I was on my way after telling MP, who gave me his blessings. I managed to obtain a bicycle right away. I had been instructed I would have to have a "laisse passer" [laissez-passer: pass] from the mairie [city hall], which was necessary [for] traveling from one place to another. I got directions on the best route to Caen and started out. I didn't know how long it would take me, but I was prepared to exert every ounce of my strength to get to my destination as fast as possible. Fortunately the weather was dry, and I estimated I had ridden two hours when I came to a bridge which I had been told would indicate I was within a kilometer of the center of Caen. It was getting dark. Two sentinels on the bridge were searching an automobile, inside and under. Thinking only of getting to the hospital as fast as possible, I had forgotton about the "laissez-passer." I had shot by like an arrow and suddenly I heard a

48. A 1915 letter from Proust to Lucien Daudet, who was suffering from bronchitis, mentions the same Dr. Alfred Chambon (1870–?) of Caen and speaks of him as a truly eminent physician. See *Corr.* 14: 227. A tribute to Dr. Chambon, published in the *Bulletin Marcel Proust,* informs us that he was the doctor who looked after summer vacationers at the Grand-Hôtel de Cabourg and in the nearby villas and châteaux. He was mobilized on August 3 and sent to hospital number 9 in Caen, which explains why Forssgren had to go to that nearby city in search of him. *Bulletin Marcel Proust,* 35 (1985): 344–47. This article also suggests that Proust might have used Chambon as a model for Dr. Boulbon in *In Search of Lost Time.*

crack of a rifle, heard something whistling by my ear. Then I realized I should have stopped and showed my identification. Another shot and something struck the bicycle. Well, too late now. I just drove on and guessed it wasn't my time. No more shots. There were some people ahead of me. I stopped and asked direction to the hospital. In a few minutes I had delivered the note to a nurse who took it to Dr. Chambon who was in the middle of an operation and sent word he would be in Cabourg le plus tôt possible [as soon as possible]. Maybe within an hour in an official chauffeur[ed] car. I was thinking, in my spent condition it would take me at least three hours to deliver the message. Ah, well, just so he gets there. Wouldn't it be nice if I could ride with him? I had my bicycle to get back and all the time in the world.

I went to a restaurant and had a well-earned dinner. It gave me time to rest up a bit. After about 45 minutes I was on my way again. It had started to rain and I started to get an awful cramp in my legs. On the bridge I was stopped by the two sentinels.

"Didn't you pass by in the other direction about an hour ago?"

"You are so right."

"Congratulations, you are a lucky man. You should have been dead or wounded. I am a fine shot. Lucky for you those people. . . ."

I showed my "laissez-passer."

"Forssgren, what kind of a name is that? Ce n'est pas français." [It isn't French.]

"Well I am not German."

I explained how I had forgotten about the identification paper. How I was on an errand of mercy and anxious to get to the hospital as fast as possible in a matter of life and death. They became very friendly when I told them I was helping to save the life of a fellow soldier, and [I] told them I was Swedish.

"Mais vous, parlez . . ." [But you speak . . .]

There they go again; I had heard it a hundred times. "You speak like a Frenchman, like a Parisien." I was beginning to enjoy the chat with these young men who became so friendly when I had explained things to them. I was asked to cross myself and promise it would be a secret between us three that I had crossed the bridge without being stopped.

"You know, we have orders to shoot to kill anyone who does not stop to identify himself. Likewise we can be shot for letting you get by the way you did." C'est la guerre. We shook hands warmly. I was slapped on my back. "Vous-etes un bon camarade, hein copin! Au revoir et bonne chance."[49]

Now it really started to pour, and me without a raincoat, getting paralyzed with cramps in my legs. No wonder, the way I had overexerted. I had to stop and rub them but it did not seem to help. What to do? Just rest I suppose. There was a big tree to the right. I got off the road and under it. It protected me from the rain somewhat, but I was soaked to the skin. I rested for perhaps a half hour until my legs began to feel normal. I was wondering what time it could be. I had failed to bring my pocket watch, and there were no wristwatches those days. I felt a chill and was seized with a fit of trembling, the ague. I thought it would go over with resuming exercise. It was pitch dark and the bicycle had no lantern. It would have been of no use anyway, the little light it would shed, except to warn "traffic" of which there was none at this hour. The rain was still coming down and the road was so muddy and slippery that I had difficulty staying upright. I could not

49. Vous êtes un bon camarade, hein copain! Au revoir et bonne chance: You're a good comrade, huh buddy! Good-bye and good luck.

ride very fast, having to be very careful. On and on I rode. I
ought to be near the fork of the road soon, where the shrine
was, Christ on a cross. I had been straining my eyes in the
dark. I was to turn right at that point. Christ showing the
right way. How symbolic! My dear religious mother used to
admonish me to let Christ guide me through life. "Always
stay on the right road, my son." Where is that shrine? I wondered if I could have passed it. I began to worry, should I turn
back? I thought I heard a faint noise. I listened, it sounded
like a trotting horse. It scared me. It might be robbers, I
thought, and I had all the money I had with me in Cabourg
on me. I quickly got off the road carrying my bicycle with me
and hid in a clump of trees. Presently I saw the black, ghostly
silhouette of a seemingly tired horse pulling a wagon on
which sat a man and a small person, probably a child. I got
back on the road. I was convinced now I had been on the
wrong road. I decided to follow at a distance. Suddenly I
thought I had been very childish. They might be some local
people that could have directed me to the shrine, but I would
have most likely scared them, popping out of nowhere in the
dark. I noticed the outlines of what I took to be farm build-
ings to my left, which I had not seen before. I was sure now I
was heading in the right direction towards the shrine. It
would be on my left. After quite a while I finally saw it.[50] By
this time my legs started bothering me worse than ever, and I
was trembling with the ague uncontrollably and felt feverish
all over, feeling a cold sweat pouring out of my body. The
cramps became unbearable. I had to stop; I couldn't go on.
Only a few more minutes and I would have been at the foot of
the cross, where I would prostrate myself. I was overwhelmed
with feelings such as I had never felt before in all my life. I

50. Forssgren typed "After quiet a while."

was convulsed with sobs. I made a superhuman effort to get to the fork of the road until I was finally there. I let the bicycle fall to the ground and threw myself before the figure of Christ. I became imbued with religious ferver and prayed like I had never done before. My mother's words came back to me. A mental picture formed in my mind of all the horribly maimed and wounded I used to see in the hospital every day. I saw the battlefield, the boy who had said war "was bloody 'ell." I saw his mangled body in the mud and slime with rain coming down in torrents, crushed by cannon wheels and war machinery. Bodies of dead and dying soldiers everywhere. Some dying cursing, others praying, dying in excrutiating pains, hopelessly waiting for alleviation, for death, release. . . . La guerre, l'incroyble folie de l'homme.[51] The whole human history having proved that no war was ever profitable except to a few tyrants, despots and warmongers and war profiteers. Tyrants with lust for power, "honor" and "glory." The unspeakable waste of money and material that could go to making the world a paradise instead of destruction and world chaos. When will man wake up and war cease? ONLY WHEN WE HAVE A WORLD BASED UPON THE PRINCIPLES OF CHRIST.

I arose feeling remarkably relieved and refreshed. My cramp had passed away although I felt feverish and was still trembling. This road to Cabourg was paved and I could make much better time. The rain had ceased and in about an hour and a half I was back at the hotel just as my cramps returned. It took a great effort to get to my room. I was an indescribable sight and was glad no one had seen me as I sneaked in the back entrance. I washed up and went to bed without seeing anyone. After a while MC knocked on my door. I said enter

51. War, the incredible folly of man. Forssgren misspells *incroyable*.

and she began to question [me]. She realized my condition and became alarmed.[52] MP who heard us came in his dressing gown and said, "Tell us about it, my son." I could hardly talk as I was shaking violently. He went to his room and called for a doctor at the hospital downstairs. He came back and told me a doctor would be up in a few minutes, and told me to rest and we would talk later. MC came back and told me to call her if there was anything I wanted. The doctor was a kindly gentleman and gave me a shot and left some pills with instructions. "You have a fine physique. You should be up in a day or so. You suffer from physical overexertion, nothing serious." I asked about Dr. Chambon and the young soldier. Dr. C[hambon] had performed the operation and it looked as though the boy might pull through, but it would be uncertain for a few days. "We hope he will live. He is a fine, strong young man. Hélas [alas], c'est la guerre. Now you rest and I shall look in on you later." I felt a great relief as the drugs started to take effect.

Shortly there was a timid knock on the door. It was MC carrying a bowl of something on a small tray. "I forgot to ask you if you had had dinner. This boullion and biscuits will do you good, and I will get you some chicken as soon as you finish the soup."

"I had a good dinner in Caen, and I am really not hungry."

It was now close to midnight.

"Vous êtes trop bonne [you are too kind], Madame Céleste."

"Why don't you call me just plain Céleste, Ernest? Your formality makes me feel so old. I am only 36."[53]

---

52. There is no trace of this episode in Céleste's memoirs or in the known letters of Proust.

53. Another indication that Forssgren's memory is poor. Céleste was

"You don't even look that old. There is something about you, something of a grande dame, that I would feel disrespectful calling you by your first name. It would seem like calling Monsieur Proust by his first name."

"Quel compliment! Vous êtes toujours si gentil [What a compliment! You are always so nice], but call me Céleste just the same."

"Eh bien, Céleste, c'est entendu alors. [Very well, Céleste, it's agreed then.] Please don't bring me any more food. This hot bouillon you so thoughtfully brought me will help me sleep. I am so dreadfully tired."

"Bonne nuit, Ernest, et dormez bien." [Good night, Ernest, and sleep well.]

"Bonne nuit, Céleste, et grand merci."

It was around noon when I woke up. My ague and cramps had left me, but I still felt feverish. I got up and bathed. I knocked on Céleste's door and rushed back to bed. I did not want her to see me in my night shirt. . . . There is something about a man's nightshirt . . . I was glad when pajamas were introduced.

"Bon jour Ernest, you look fine; you must have slept well."

"Merci, chère Céleste, I have."

"MP has talked to your doctor. He says you must rest for at least two days. MP will see you after you have had your lunch. It will be sent up shortly."

At 1 o'clock MP came to see me, dressed as usual in his heavy woolen dressing gown[,] and sat down in my easy chair.

"Tell me about it, you young adventurer."

I told him the essential details, omitting the emotional

---

twenty-two years old, only three years older than Forssgren. Proust's letters show that everyone who met her at the time was struck by her youthful beauty.

dramatics and leaving out the bridge insident, of course. He had brought me papers with the latest war news and some books to read.

"I shall not bother you now, but I'll look in later in the day. You must rest all you can. The doctor says you should be up and well in a couple of days. I shall have something for you to do then. See you later. By the way we will have to postpone the journey back to Paris for another week or so."

I thanked him for bringing me the reading matter. The war news was encouraging as compared to previous news. We would definitely be able to go back to Paris for good. I was wondering where he had got the books, but as he had friends who were living in Cabourg permanently, I surmised some one of them had brought them over, knowing about the limited amount of baggage we were able to bring with us from Paris. What a kind man MP is. I had told him I had just started reading <u>Count of Monte Christo</u> [*sic*] when I had to leave Prince Orloff's. He had brought me a volume, as well as other A[lexandre]. Dumas books. I had told him I could read his works over and over and that he was my favorite writer.[54] I am really going to enjoy my convalescence. The days passed almost too quickly. My heart was full of love and gratitude towards MP and Céleste, the two most lovable people I had ever known.[55]

I was up and well, and after taking care of some work for MP, I went back to my hospital duties. I went to see the young man whose life I had tried to help save. It was still doubtful he would pull through, but the doctors seemed hopeful.

54. The translator changed "reading over and over" to "le lire tout d'une traite": read him all at one go.

55. Céleste could not abide Forssgren. Had he been bedridden and required such attention from her and from Proust, it seems unlikely that she would have omitted this reversal of fortune from her memoirs.

That evening I was playing checkers with MP when MC knocked on his door. She brought a note for MP which he proceeded to read after making excuses to me, the typical Proust politeness. Whether you were a servant or an homme du monde, it didn't seem to make any difference to him.[56] After reading it he handed it over for me to read. There was another knock from MC's door. Before Céleste had time to open it I had thrown the note on MP's bed. MC gave MP a message she had forgotten and withdrew.

"Why did you do that?" MP asked.

"It should be obvious to you," I said.

"Quel tact, quel tact inouïle [inouï: What tact, what unheard of tact], from a young man of twenty years. You know, you are a remarkable young man."

"No disrespect, MP, but I think you exaggerate too much."

"I know why," he said, "but tell me anyway."[57]

"It is not quite comme il faut [proper] for a servant to be on such intimate terms with his master that he can read his private correspondence, and it is best not to announce it to others."

"Ernest, you are no servant, never can or will be. You are my secretary, companion and confidant, no less, not quite a servant. This time you are going to have to [accept]," he said,

56. This is the picture one gets of Proust from those who have left descriptions of him. It varies sharply from the stereotypical one, largely discredited by now, one hopes, of him as an effete snob. He often preferred the company of young men from the working class to that of his male acquaintances who belonged to *le gratin*, the upper crust of Parisian society. See Carter, *Proust in Love*.

57. The translator has altered the meaning here from Proust's "I know why you did that but I want to hear you say it," to "'Je ne vois pas très bien pourquoi,' répliqua-t-il quand même": "'I don't very well see why,' he replied anyway."

as he pulled out the drawer of his nightstand and took out a 500 franc note and held it out to me.

"Now you cannot say you haven't earned it."

"Get thee behind me, Satan," I thought. "You know we have an agreement that you are not to tempt me like that, Monsieur."

"Yes, but you have earned it, especially volunteering your work in the hospital."

"Don't forget it is volunteer work, MP, and the salary you are paying for the little work I do is more than adequate."

"I think you are very foolish; you are carrying idealism too far. You should be more practical. I think you have earned it in many ways, especially considering your ordeal on your trip to Caen. Money means nothing to me, but a lot to you to-wards your ambitious career."

With tongue in cheek, so to speak, and a sly smile, I said, "Do you candidly think I have earned it?"

"Of course you have."

"I wonder if I should accept it, since you think I have earned it, and you are rich, and it would mean so much to me. Perhaps I need to learn to be more practical. On second thought I think I will accept it."

"So you decided to be sensible; that's good."

He looked at me rather quizzically as he handed me the 500 franc note.

I thought I detected a nuance of disappointment.

Every man has a price depending on how much . . . He suggested I show him some card tricks for a change. I showed him one I had never done [for him?] before. Although it is quite simple it always amazes everyone.

"You must be in league with the devil. I have always thought you were an extraordinary young man."

He looked almost alarmed. I decided to teach him it.

"In just a minute you can perform the same trick."

I showed him how it was done and he started to laugh heartily. It did my heart good to see him in such a jolly mood.

"Ernest, you are a tonic," he said, as he stretched out his arms to embrace me. "I have never seen a man such as you."[58]

Céleste knocked again; it was time for his dinner and I went down for mine.

The next morning I did my turn in the hospital, greeted very cordially by everyone including my doctor who said, "You are looking fine young man. We are glad to have you back with us."

I looked in at my soldier boy. He was improving and wanted to shake hands. He had been told I was the angel of mercy who had fetched Doctor Chambon. At noon I went for a swim and had lunch. I reported to MP who had an errand for me in town. I told him I had some errands for myself also and would he mind if I was an hour late. Of course not.

After doing the errand for MP, I went to the local depart-

58. Is this true? Was Proust falling in love with Forssgren or did he simply desire him? Proust had by now largely recovered from the tragic death, only four months earlier, of his beloved former secretary-chauffeur Alfred Agostinelli. After returning from Cabourg in the fall of 1914, Proust wrote a long letter to Reynaldo Hahn about the process of grieving and forgetting that reads like a draft for similar sentiments expressed by the Narrator mourning Albertine's death. In that letter, he says of his lack of fidelity to the recently deceased Agostinelli: "So if I had a few weeks of relative inconstancy at Cabourg, don't condemn me as fickle but blame the person who was incapable of deserving fidelity." See SL 3: 280–81. Could the person with whom he was "inconstant" have been Forssgren or some other young man at Cabourg? Proust's fascination with Forssgren is proven by his fruitless attempt to see Forssgren during the latter's return to Paris for a brief visit in 1922. Forssgren describes this missed rendezvous at the end of the memoirs. For more about Proust and Agostinelli, see chapter 8, "Grieving and Forgetting," in Carter, Proust in Love.

ment store where I was attended [to] by a saleslady who had decided I was English and wanted to display her knowledge of English. It consisted of four words, such as she pronounced them, and I was satisfied it was her entire command of the language. I noticed the prices were about 20% higher here than in Paris and asked about it. She completely ignored my French I was so proud of, and kept repeating like a parrot: "Becose off zuh vaahr." Cabourg was a popular tourist resort of the English.[59] So, "becose off zuh vaahr" I decided to add 100 francs of my own to MP's 500 francs and proceeded to buy up the store. I bought cigarettes, tobacco, zig-zag papers to roll it in, cigars, pipes, decks of cards, checker and chess sets, books, magazines, etc., for 600 francs. I had to make two trips to deliver to the hospital, with the compliments of Monsieur Marcel Proust, the writer. There were still no taxis for hire.

The next morning I did my turn in the hospital, had my dip and lunch as usual. It was 4 o'clock and I was playing checkers with MP when there was a knock on the door leading to the corridor outside. I looked at MP who nodded. I went to the door to open it and saw a delegation of four ladies who requested to see MP. I motioned them to enter. It was headed by the chief matron of the hospital, Countess de M., a friend of MP. It was known that MP would receive visitors at that hour and in bed.[60] The Countess knew that and it was

59. Because of their relative proximity to England, the seaside resorts of Normandy such as Cabourg, Deauville, Trouville, and Houlgate had long been favorites of British tourists.

60. This scene also seems to be an invention. Proust had a strict rule about not receiving female visitors when in bed. Furthermore, Céleste says that at Cabourg he received no guests that she recalled. Her memory seems validated on this point by Proust himself, who mentions in a letter that two distinguished men of the nobility called on him at the Grand-Hôtel— Counts Henri Greffulhe and Montesquiou—but he declined to receive them because he felt unwell. *Corr.* 13: 309. Céleste remembers this also, ex-

presumed she had explained to the other ladies the situation. After they had entered I was going to retire tactfully, but MP motioned me to stay. The Countess greeted MP very effusively and introduced the other ladies, also of the nobility as indicated by the introduction. "Monsieur Proust, we have come to thank you for your wonderfully generous gesture. It was indeed thoughtful of you to make such appropriate gifts. Just what we needed."

"Qu'est que c'est que ça? Je'n comprend rien du tout."[61]

"Ah, MP[,] la modestie et la générocité de MP est bien connue . . . Mais je vous jure . . ."[62]

He glanced at me and I had to lower my eyelids to hide my guilt.

"Mesdames, permettez-moi de vous présenter Monsieur Ernest, mon secrétaire. Voilà le coupable."[63]

MP also had a little sense of humor. He proceeded to wring a full confession from me. He explained he had wanted to reward me for offering my services in the hospital and told

---

cept that she believed that it was the comtesse Greffulhe and Robert de Montesquiou. Albaret, *Monsieur Proust,* 32. What Forssgren says in the "Summary" about the rooms at Cabourg and Proust's activities reflects more accurately what we know about the writer's habits: "We had a suite of three rooms adjoining all connecting with each other, doors between each room. M.P.'s room first, nearest the elevator, then Madame Céleste's room next to his, and then mine. If he had visitors after I left him, usually 8 or 9 o'clock, I knew nothing about it. He would always have M.C. call me when he wanted me, and he would always tell me when he wanted me to leave."

61. Qu'est-ce que c'est que ça? Je n'y comprends rien du tout: What's that? I have no idea what you're talking about.

62. La modestie et la générosité de Monsieur Proust sont bien connues: Monsieur Proust's modesty and generosity are well known. But I swear to you . . .

63. Ladies, allow me to introduce Monsieur Ernest, my secretary. He's the culprit.

them about the Caen incident and that this is what I had done with the money.[64] The gifts were from me[,] he told them.[65] He told them I was Swedish.

"Oh, how wonderful," the ladies enthused. "And he is such a capable and friendly young man, so thoughtful and helpful, the wounded all love him," said the Countess de M. When the ladies heard I was Swedish they became very interested and started to ask me about my country and what I thought Sweden's final stand would be in the war and [about] the rumors about the possibility of Sweden entering the war on the side of Germany, hoping they were unfounded.

"You know we French are sort of related to your country; our illustrious Maréchal Bernadotte became your king and our wonderful Désirée, your queen.[66] We do hope Sweden does not join up with Germany."

"There is very little danger of that. My country has too much friendship and admiration for La Belle Franca [la Belle France: beautiful France]," I told them.

The visit lasted only a few minutes, there being only two chairs and it wasn't expected of all that nobility to sit on his bed. In fact MP had been quite embarrassed, but he knew the Countess had explained things.

When the ladies had left, MP looked at me in mock anger and said, "You hypocrite!" He got out of bed and threw his

64. The word *that* in this sentence was originally rendered "that that," but the duplicate word was stricken by hand.

65. We have seen Proust state in several letters that the gifts were from him. Had they been from Forssgren, he would certainly have acknowledged the fact and been extremely pleased with the young man. Such generosity in this case—depleting his money supply, which, according to Céleste, forced him to leave Cabourg and return to Paris—is entirely in keeping with everything we know about Proust and his profligate way with money.

66. The translator changed "maréchal" to "général," but Forssgren's title is correct.

arms around me and kissed me on the cheek. ["]Sorbonne will have to wait unless you quit being so stubborn.["][67]

MC must have been rather curious of what was going on as she must have heard all the talking, her room adjoining, separated only by a door.[68] She made herself an errand and MP enlightened her with the whole story, how he had thought I should be rewarded for what I must have endured taking the note to Caen in the rain and getting sick as I did, and my volunteer work in the hospital, and then I had gone and "squandered" the money as I had done.[69]

The days passed routinely. MP was visiting the hospital, wanting to correct a "grave" error. His friendly, charming, encouraging speech to the wounded soldiers included a full repudiation as to the gifts and that the idea was that of Monsieur Ernest, his secrétaire. "It was his way of discreetly expressing his professed love and admiration for La Franca, its people and, as he put it, the world's most beautiful, cultural and elegant language. As you know he has volunteered his services in this hospital besides working for me. He has vowed that if his country, La Suède, should enter the war on the side of Germany as rumored, he shall immediately join

67. Forssgren apparently intended to attribute this line to Proust but forgot to enclose it in quotes.

68. We notice in Forssgren's little play that every time Proust makes an overture towards intimacy, Céleste comes barging into the room. She never dared enter his room unless summoned. (See Albaret, *Monsieur Proust*, 303.) By this invention, Forssgren can exaggerate the adulation and intimacy shown him by Proust and yet shield himself from the potential accusation of having been too intimate. As an additional cover, Forssgren—in the text that follows—gives himself a girlfriend at Cabourg. This sole mention in the memoirs of his having ever been interested in women is rather unconvincing.

69. Proust would have indeed been impressed by such a gesture had it taken place and would not have considered the money squandered.

the French forces. As I know this rash, adventurous young man, he will probably do it before then."

There was an outburst of applause, hurrahs, bravos and vive Monsieur Ernest, upon which I shouted vive La France, and led into la Marseillaise. I had taken first prize at the French language school at the Swedish church, 9 rue Guyot, in reciting it.[70] I had recited it for MP once who said it was "tout à fait comme Sacha Guitry," the well known actor.[71]

Came the time to depart for Paris and our baggage was packed and loaded on the pushcart the hotel porter was conveying to la gare. We had a few minutes before train time, and much to my embarrassment there came Marie, whom I had been seeing clandestinely (I had already said good-bye) for a last tearful good-bye. She was whispering that her husband was returning from a three month sea voyage, being a seaman.

She told me, "I am leaving for La [Le] Havre tomorrow."

"You . . . you never told me you were married . . ." ah these women . . .

MP looked at me with a twinkle in his eye. And there was Céleste, what would she think?

"I take it you have not been too bored in Cabourg," this from MP, smiling insinuatingly.

This time we traveled first class and very comfortably. The trip was very enjoyable as we traveled through beautiful country.[72] In about 5 to 6 hours we arrived in Paris. We were

70. Église luthérienne norvégienne et suédoise (the Norwegian and Swedish Lutheran Church). This street, now renamed rue Médéric, is in the seventeenth arrondissement, near the Parc de Monceau.

71. Sacha Guitry (1885–1957) was an actor, playwright, and filmmaker.

72. Forssgren's memory seems faulty here. Céleste in her memoirs and Proust in his letters both write about a terrible asthma crisis that seized him as the train approached Mézidon and about Céleste's heroic efforts to talk her way into the baggage car to retrieve his medicine, which she, being new

delighted to notice that Paris seemingly had not been affected by the war, that we could notice. This time we were
able to get a taxi although they were very scarce.[73]

I was anxious to get some things from my baggage at
Prince Orloff's. I did not know if there would be anyone there
but the concierge. There had not been any word from M.
Pralon, the secrétaire of the Prince, so I took it they were still
in Pau. I had written M. Pralon and given him my address in
Cabourg. As I arrived at 45–47 Rue Sai[n]t Dominique I was
greeted very warmly by the concierge and his wife.[74] They
had just had a letter from M. Pralon, the secretary, saying
that the Prince would be back with his entourage in two
weeks and the mansion would be opened up and, of course, I
would be coming back. I was going to be needed as most of
the men had been drafted. I was allowed to go to my room to
get the things I needed. I told them to convey the message to
M. Pralon that he could reach me at M. Proust's. He had the
phone number and the address.

Oh, that depressing room, still smelling of fumigation.
How would I ever get used to it? MP used to make his fumi-

---

on the job, had forgotten to pack separately and bring in the train car with
them. Had Forssgren been the hero of this episode, he certainly would have
recounted it. Perhaps he simply forgot this incident. See Albaret, *Monsieur
Proust,* 36–37, and *Corr.* 13: 304, 306, where, in a letter to Madame Albert
Nahmias, Proust talks about the determined efforts of his "valet de chambre" to retrieve the medication. This is presumably because he did not want
her to know he was traveling with a young woman as his servant. As we have
seen, he had expressed these concerns regarding propriety to Céleste after
she had gamely offered to disguise herself as a man for the train ride to
Cabourg. See *SL* 3: 276.

73. The French excerpts break here and resume only toward the end of
the memoirs, when Forssgren describes his return to Paris in 1922.

74. As we have seen, Prince Orloff lived at 45 rue Saint-Dominique, in
the seventh arrondissement, near the Church of the Invalides.

gation almost daily in Cabourg, while I was in the hospital, but it was nothing like this. Perhaps due to the fact that the windows faced the ocean and were kept open an hour every day. There was always the electric heater drying the room if there was too much dampness in the air. As I had hardly spent any time in the apartment everything was new to me, or should I say old. The furniture consisted of very elegant antiques mostly. There was the foyer off which was a cabinet de toilette with a washbowl, MP's bedroom and a very elegant salon. Céleste's and my room[s] were in the back separated by a bathroom, facing a gloomy courtyard. The address as mentioned in the beginning was 88 Blvd. Haussmann, not far from the famous opéra de Paris, in the center of Paris.

The routine of work here was quite different from Cabourg, a lot more of it. It took a little time to organize things. My duty would be to do the shopping as Céleste would do the cooking and most of the cleaning.[75] As MP was on his light and delicate diet, the question of meals was very simple. I would have to deliver a lot of notes to various friends of his, as it was considered more polite than telephoning. As a matter of fact the phone was used very little in France in those days, mostly in emergencies. I went through MP's wardrobe to see what had to be done. After all I was his valet. What much else was there for me to do? I could never stand idleness. I suggested he move into the salon for a few days so I could give his room a thorough going over. But as he thought of his fumigations, he thought it would smell up the salon, to which I agreed with him. We compromised on the foyer, as it would only be for a day or two. He wanted to call in some women to do the work, but I insisted on doing it.

---

75. Céleste had not yet learned to cook, but she did do the cleaning, which makes what follows in Forssgren's account seem dubious.

"At Prince Orloff's I had to do cleaning every morning, so I am an expert. I want to earn my salary, and since my work as your secretary is practically nonexistent as yet, what else can I do[?] I can still play checkers with you and read to you as we did at Cabourg when you feel like it. I take it you will set to work on your writing seriously, now that you are back in Paris. You will get back to yourself, MP. In Cabourg you seemed rather out of your element, so to speak. Aren't you glad to be back in Paris now that winter is here, Monsieur?"[76]

"Ernest, I cannot see you cleaning; it does not suit you. It will spoil the picture I have of you. You would look ridiculous. I want you to look up some concern that contracts for that kind of work. There are some in Paris. And I want you to look up a painting firm to do the kitchen and your rooms as well as the bathroom. It all needs doing I have noticed.[77] And I would like you to see about a typewriter. Try to get brochures of different ones and prices. I want you to start to practice

76. It is difficult to imagine any servant of the era talking in such a manner to his employer, and especially to Marcel Proust. The season was still fall.

77. Proust would never have tolerated such a "going over," and he certainly would not have moved anywhere, let alone to the foyer. Forssgren must have left Proust's service shortly after the return from Cabourg. He has either forgotten or is inventing. According to Céleste, Proust had a crew clean his apartment every year during his stay in Cabourg. In 1914, upon Proust's return to Paris, the crew was just beginning to work. Proust was so tired from his asthma attack and the trip that he sent them away. Albaret, *Monsieur Proust*, 37. Proust had a horror of having any workmen nearby and certainly would not have engaged cleaners or painters or anyone at a time that would disrupt his schedule, nor would he have tolerated the fumes of either. Proust does not mention such cleaning and painting in the letters written after the return to Paris. One reason that Céleste's complete lack of culinary skills mattered little to Proust is that most often prepared food was brought in, usually from Larue's restaurant and later the Ritz hotel, because Proust could not tolerate cooking odors in the apartment.

typewriting as soon as possible. I am going to do a great deal of writing from now on. You will have enough to do as my secretary. That charming little story you wrote about you and your sister getting lost in the woods, picking berries, the thunderstorm that frightened you, and you saving your sister from drowning—it is such a charming little story I would like to have it published. When you wrote it did you have to consult the La Rousse [Larousse] (dictionary) for the spelling? I noticed that it was perfect."[78]

"No, I did not. That is the great advantage of the Latin languages; after you have learned all the rules thoroughly, you need never consult a dictionary, like you constantly have to do with the idiotic English spelling.[79] Once you have learned the orthography of a Latin language and its grammatical rules you have no need of a dictionary.[80] As for the English language, it reflects the character and nature of its people. Like the French reflects a refined, cultured and artistic people. It is said that language reflects a nation's psyche, its soul and character. English reflects a conservative nation

78. We can see from this document that Forssgren was capable of misspelling the simplest, most common French words—even "France" itself. There is no evidence that Proust sought to have a story by Forssgren published.

79. Forssgren seems to be unaware that Proust had published an annotated translation of John Ruskin's *The Bible of Amiens* (1904) and had done the same for parts of Ruskin's *Sesame and Lilies* (1905). A conversation about English versus French with Proust would have been quite different from the one Forssgren relates.

80. This is nonsense, of course. Even Proust used a dictionary, usually the Littré, which he considered the standard one. He would have corrected Forssgren's absurd remarks. While one can argue that French is, relatively speaking, closer to being a phonetic language than English, the spelling of French words is much less predictable than Forssgren claims. His own frequent mistakes prove the point. I am assuming that he typed the text, or at least proofread it if someone else typed it.

reluctant of change, and though the language like all languages has gone through changes, the English have been slow in following up with reform in spelling. As an example, the obsolete GH was the Saxon's equivalent of the German CH, but was eventually slurred over and dropped, but the spelling retained. The Scotch humorous, 'it is a brah bright moonlight night tonight' is an example of the correct spelling and the original pronunciation."[81]

"Where did you learn all that?" MP asked.

"At Prince Orloff's I came across a volume dealing with the origin of language. I looked it over rather superficially. I am not too well versed, but I shall take it up again in connection with my further studies."

The next day I went out to carry out MP's instructions and arranged to have two women to do housecleaning the following Monday. I had difficulty locating a painter and had to let it go until another day. I got some brochures on typewriters, with prices marked.[82] Awfully expensive, I thought. The following day I went to see about a painter. It took me near Prince Orloff's and I decided to call there again as there was something I needed which I had forgot the first time. The concierge handed me a letter which had just arrived. It gave me quite a shock. It contained orders for me to return to Sweden to fulfill my military duty. I had to be back in Sweden within two months or as soon as traveling conditions allowed.

81. In his recent highly acclaimed novel *Atonement* (New York: N. A. Talese/Doubleday, 2002), the British writer Ian McEwan uses a version of this same sentence as an example of Cockney: "'It's a braw bricht moonlicht nicht the nicht,' Nettle called out in Cockney" (205).

82. According to Céleste, Proust sold the typewriter, used by Agostinelli during his tenure as secretary, to the director of the restaurant Larue, located not far from boulevard Haussmann. She used to see the typewriter next to the cashier when she went there to pick up food. See Albaret, *Monsieur Proust*, 233, 96.

How was my address obtained? It could only be through the Swedish church where I was registered. All men of military age were to report back in Sweden. This completely changed the picture. Later I went to the reading room at the Swedish church and met an acquaintance my age who had gotten the same order.[83] He told me he would never take a chance having to fight against France, feeling the same as I about this great country. He would, like me, fight on the side of France, if Sweden should enter the war on Germany's side, as it continued to be rumored. But, he had found out something that sent my hopes up. We could emigrate to America. I had told MP the day before that I was developing a guilt complex, the way people were staring at me as if asking why wasn't I in uniform? It made me feel like "un lâche" [a coward]. I ought to join up. I have no right to enjoy the hospitality of France while the flower of her manhood had to sacrifice their lives. I had said I thought I would join the ambulance corps. I felt I could never kill anyone, but there was a need of infirmiers [male nurses] and ambulance drivers. MP disuaded me but thought it was a noble idea, and [said that] I should wait a while and see what Sweden would do.

When I gave MP the news about the order to return to Sweden he was greatly upset. This then would mean an early parting of the ways. We spent a great deal of time together discussing the new development. Was there something I could do to postpone the return to Sweden? I told him there was nothing. It could possibly mean Sweden's early entry into the war, a thing I dreaded most. I told him about the surprising fact that I could emigrate to America. His face lit up.

"That is what you must do then," he said. "And if the war does not last too long, you can come back, and in the mean-

<hr>

83. Forssgren typed an otiose apostrophe after the word *reading*.

while I will arrange for your entry into the University.[84] There will be a better chance for you then, with so many lost in the war."

["]One man's death, another man's bread,["] I thought.

"I still think I ought to join the abulance [*sic*] corps."

"No, to go to America is the best solution for you. As Sweden is not in the war yet you don't have to feel like a deserter. It would be the best for both of us. I shall really need you after the war, and you can work for me part time while you study at the University."

Just the thought that had entered my mind at our first interview.

Two days later I got a note from M. Pralon, to come to see him. I knew just what that meant. M. Pralon greeted me in a very friendly manner, and went right to the point.

"When can you come back? Right away I hope. I came ahead of the Prince to open up the house. As you probably understand, the household staff is reduced to almost half with so many men drafted. When full staffed it consisted of approximately 22 men and 6 women.[85] I shall have to restaff as many as I can, but it will be difficult to get men."

If it was not for the order to return to Sweden, it had been my intention to give M. Pralon notice that I was leaving the service of the Prince and devote my time with MP. I told M. Pralon about the order to return.

"It does not surprise me. There are those rumors about Sweden joining with Germany. How soon will you have to leave?"

84. This seems an unlikely promise for Proust to make, especially to a foreign domestic with no high school diploma. Perhaps he offered to somehow facilitate Forssgren's attempt to enroll.

85. Although this sentence is within the quotation marks, Forssgren apparently intended it to be an aside.

"Within two months or sooner," I told him. "There will be difficulty getting there with all the blockades and sinking of ships. Overland is, of course, impossible. I probably will have to start early by way of England."

"It would be of great help if you could come and stay as long as you can, until I can replace you. The Prince will be very sorry to hear this. He is very fond of you and as you know he has raised your salary to 175 francs a month, something unheard of."

I told him of MP and I could not just up and leave him abruptly, as we had just returned from Cabourg.

"Try and do the best you can. You know it was our understanding you were to come back as soon as the Prince would open up his house again."

"I shall do what I can and be back here as soon as I can arrange things."

I did not tell him about my tentative America plans. Things were not the same at MP's anymore. MP looked sad and discouraged. He had told Céleste, who had shed some tears.[86] We went ahead with the cleaning and painting. A week later I moved back to Prince Orloff's.[87] I had promised I would be back and see if there would be anything I could do for him [Proust] every day I was off duty. He was grateful. We had the mutual understanding I was going to quit Prince Orloff for good and come and work for him, but subsequent developments changed all that. I had by now definitely decided I would go to America and had applied for [a] passport, and much to my joy I was told it would be issued shortly and

86. This is simply laughable. Céleste, like Françoise in the novel, viewed any other servant as an intruder. We have already seen her mocking Forssgren's conceit and describe his uselessness as a domestic.

87. Forssgren did so most likely because Proust no longer had need of his services.

I would be notified. I had been back at Prince Orloff's about two weeks when I got notice from the Swedish legation to report for my passport. There were some formalities and some papers to sign. I had inquired about passage to America and found there was no difficulty about passage as there were not many traveling due to the submarine scare. I would have to go to Calais and cross over to England on one of the small boats crossing the channel ever [sic] day. They were not bothered by submarines or blockades, being too unimportant. I had discarded and given away some things, so I had only two valises to carry.

The time for departure came. The Prince asked to see me. M. Pralon had told him about the choice I had of going back to Sweden or of going to America. Of course, the latter was fraught with danger, that I knew, but it was the lesser of two evils. The Prince was very friendly, even asked me to sit down. We chatted for quite a while until the Prince finally stretched out his arm and I rose and we shook hands warmly.

"Adieu Prince, que Dieu vous garde."

"Merci et de mame [même] à vous, mon brave garçon."[88]

I received a very fine reference signed by the Prince himself.

The hardest part remained. MP was out of bed in his dressing gown. We talked at great length about future plans. I had to promise, of course, to come back after the war only if Sweden stayed neutral; otherwise I would be in it myself one way or another on the side of France. There had been speculation of what America would do. If she eventually entered the fracas, it would be on the allied side, and then I would join the A.E.F., but only if Sweden entered, he amended.[89]

88. "Good-bye, Prince, may God keep you." "Thank you and the same to you, my brave young lad."

89. Does A.E.F. stand for American Expeditionary Forces? If so, the

"You know how much I need you, and how much you need me. We can be great help to one another. You know I can never replace you. Your honesty and reliability, your warm personality, and not to mention your wonderful sense of humor."

MP looked haggard, tense and emotional, and I felt the same. We embraced and we both burst into tears.

"Adieu, cher Ernest, que Dieu vous bénisse, au revoir et bon retour."

"Adieu mon cher maître, que Dieu vous bénisse et garde."[90]

Then came the tearful, emotional farewell with Céleste. Was [sic] there any more wonderful people than these two? I was taking the train at Gare du Nord for Calais. I was carrying my two valises. There was plenty of time until the train's departure. The strangest, saddest feeling came over me. When will I ever see this wonderful city again, the world's most beautiful? This great country, La France, the cradle of liberty, where man's first real quest for freedom originated. The charming, friendly, unaffected, natural people. A sincere people without conceit, confirming: "none so modest as the truly great." La France, the country where, at last, I found true friendship and understanding, and APPRECIATION. VIVE TOUJOURS LA FRANCE! [May France live forever!]

I arrived in London late that night without insidents. I checked my baggage at the station. I was already acquainted with London and had no difficulty finding a hotel for the

---

A.E.F. did not exist in 1914, when this conversation allegedly took place. Perhaps Forssgren was anticipating that America would send forces to aid the French and British.

90. "Good-bye dear Ernest, may God bless you, good-bye and have a safe return." "Good-bye my dear master, may God bless you and keep you."

night. I got up early and had breakfast and promenaded around until the steam ship offices opened. I went to the White Star Line where there was a boat leaving for New York in three days, $60, second class, the "Cymric." I decided to see what the Cunard line had to offer. They had a boat, the "Transylvania" leaving Liverpool the next day, a new boat. Fare $67, second class. I decided to take IT. I inquired about [a] train for Liverpool and was told there was one leaving in two hours. I decided to take it when I was told I could go aboard the ship as soon as I reached Liverpool. I arrived there in a few hours and took a taxi to the boat. It was an exciting sight. I had never seen such a large ship, and so beautiful. I was able to put my valises in my cabin right away. I would be sharing it with three other men. The ship fascinated me no end. It was fun to explore it from one end to the other. Its weight was 16000 dpt. I was told. It was evening and dinner-time. I was pleasantly surprised at the wonderful food, and I spent a pleasant evening in the ship's salon and made a few acquaintances. I was worried about the money I was carrying and asked a steward for advice. He told me to deposit it with the purser and get a receipt, which I did and my worries were over. There was [sic] only two of us in the cabin, since the ship was not leaving until morning.

It was noon the next day that the ship started moving and we were on our way to the great, mysterious land of great promise. I felt an exilirating excitement. We were headed for the land of liberty I had read so much about. We were now four in the cabin, very nice chaps. It looked as though we were going to get along fine. We were having lunch and it looked as though the ship was carrying a capacity load of pas-sengers. Everyone seemed in a gay mood. No atmosphere of fear. We were escorted for four days by two English cruisers. On the third day there was news that the "Cymric" was sunk

Ernest Forssgren as he looked when Proust hired him as his
valet de chambre in September 1914.

Proust's inscription on the copy of *Du côté de chez Swann* that he gave Ernest Forssgren in 1914 reads "A Ernst Forssgren, en témoignage de ma parfaite estime et de mon cordial souvenir. Marcel Proust" —To Ernst Forssgren, as proof of my perfect esteem and fond memory. Marcel Proust.

The inscription on the back of the
photograph reads "À Ernst Forssgren,
amical souvenir, MP"—To Ernst
Forssgren, fond memories, MP.

Forssgren's photocopy of the note left for him at the Riviera Hotel.

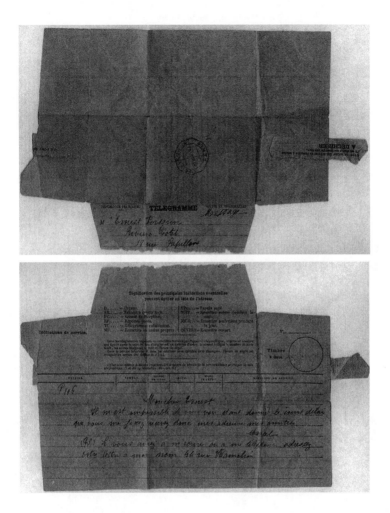

The date on this telegram, September 1, 1922, is a clue to the
chronology of Proust's activities in August and September and the date
of the "mysterious visit" to the Riviera Hotel. The telegram, addressed to
Ernest Forssgren at the Riviera Hotel reads "Mon cher Ernest, Il m'est
impossible de vous voir étant donné le court délai que vous me fixez
donc mes adieux. Mes amitiés, Marcel (PS) Si vous aviez à m'écrire ou à
me téléphoner adressez votre lettre à mon nom 44, rue Hamelin."—My
dearest Ernest, It is impossible for me to see you given the short notice
you have given me, therefore, farewell. Cordially yours, Marcel. (PS) If
you have to write or phone me send your letter in my name to 44 rue
Hamelin.

THE AMERICAN STANDARD PHONETIC ALPHABET

Originated and first introduced, suggested and proposed, in the year 1917, as solution towards a spelling reform of the AMERICAN LANGUAGE By: Ernest A. Forssgren.

It is offered for comparison with the english 44 letter alphabet proposed by the english, as depicted on this page, and speaks for itself.

The AMERICAN STANDARD PHONETIC ALPHABET. For the sake of simplicity, uniformity and consistency, the letter E as pronounced in latin is chosen, as the "consonant-vowel" for ALL the consonants. Thus the consonants are: Be, Ce*, De, Fe, Ge*, He, Je*, Ke, Le, Me, Ne, Pe, Qe*, Re, Se, Te, Ve, We, Xe*, Ze. **Vowels: A, open as in fat. AA, closed as in far. AE, as in air. E, open as in den. EE, closed as in deer. I, short as in pin. II, long as in peer. O, open as in pot. OO, closed as in poor. U*, open as in nut. UU, pronounced as in russian. **Oe**, as in nook, long as in noon. **oe** in italian, making one letter do for two*. Oe*, always hard as in go. Je*, always as in je*; also serving for the "Eoft" Q. Ge* as in she. Xe*, as in there, thin*. The letter in rude, rule, true, has only one single sound, e.g. as in rude, rule, true. There are NO double consonants.

NB. To make a language 100% phonetic, ALL letters and symbols can have but one pronunciation. THE AMERICAN STANDARD PHONETIC ALPHABET is 100% phonetic as will be seen. When properly understood. No need to consult dictionaries. It covers and includes two vowels, viz: the closed and the long vowel pronunciation is used.

The italian language, acknowledged one of the world's most melodious, most distinct and most beautiful of all languages, has only 21 letters and no waste, consisting of seven vowels, viz: A, E, I, O, U, with E and O open and closed and total of seven vowels. THE REASON. Under no consideration should there be any more letters added to the already existing alphabet. In reciting the AMERICAN STANDARD ALPHABET the closed and long vowel pronunciation is used.

As there are a number of more or less perceptible vowel-sound variations, depending on locality, it is suggested that a committee of AMERICAN language experts be appointed to standardize the AMERICAN vowel and vowel-sounds. Under no circumstances should there be more than 13 vowels which this proposed phonetic alphabet provides. On the peculiarity of the AMERICAN language calls for, which peculiarity, too, the AMERICAN language, with other european languages. The Hawaiian language, noted for charm, beauty and clarity has an alphabet consisting of ONLY twelve letters, which goes to show that too many letters in a given alphabet only creates confusion and clutters up the language.

A bizarre new 44-character alphabet could soon be teaching your child to read and write. The October JOURNAL tells ry have found this past year with the new I.T.A. (Initial Teaching Alphabet, ce below). Now far past its experimental stage, I.T.A. is the official teaching alphabet in Great Britain, may soon be in use here as well. Last year Britain's I.T.A. teaches faster because its symbols correspond more closely to the actual sounds t our language than do the 26 letters i present use. So, evidence showed, at the children who learn to read and write with the aid of this longer alphabet et are later able to make the shift to ve shorter traditional alphabet quickly and easily. You should know the pros and cons of this amazing departure in machine which may soon affect your children.

OVER

In these modern, hectic times the trend seems, more and more, to be towards speed, efficiency, practicability and elimination of waste of time and motion. For this reason it will not be long before America has adopted the metric system in its entirety. Indeed, most of the american industry has already come a good way in this direction. It is rather ironical that the world's richest and most advanced country should be 100 years behind the rest of the world in this respect. It must be admitted however that America has the finest money system, because it is based on the metric system. It is ahead of other countries in the fact that money bills are all of the same size fitting into uniform pocket books without having to be folded.

In this connection, is it not time to do something about one of the world's most important mediums of communication, namely the AMERICAN LANGUAGE, making it 100% phonetic like most other languages, and thus making it more available to the rest of the world? With even greater urgency than the metric system. In fact, one of the world's greatest, most crying needs today. It would have a tremendously beneficial effect upon the entire world. The PHONETIC AMERICAN would enable americans to learn foreign languages with ease; and vice versa, something the english, with their decadent "language" never can. Only the english dictionaries have the absurd symbols on the margin of the pages indicating the "correct" pronunciation. In no other language is this necessary.

The english bible for instance, gives the same symbols, resulting in pronouncing the letter I, in particular, as AI instead of the latin I, (EE), Uriah, Yewraiah, instead of Ou ree ah, Goliath, Golaiit instead of Go iee at, etc ad infinitum. No, not infi naitum. The same confusion as regards the letter E. These two vowels, E and I constitute the most flagrant english corruption of the alphabet, and cause the greatest confusion. It is most timely and urgent for americans to realize that they must do something about THEIR language to suit themselves, and not the english.

Every person has to, now and again, consult the english dictionary, for spelling and pronunciation of english words, all through life. Waeras it taeks e laif taim ty lurn and rimember hau ty spel and pronauns inglig wurds, it wil teik onli minits ty lurn xu speling and pronunsieixun ov xu FONETIK AMERIKAN. Nou niid ty ever konsult e dikgonaeri.

Ai rest an artikl in xu S.P. Eksaminer ov 6/5/68 abaut e kurnel Manly B. Gibson, e ritaird armi kurnel (colonel) kurnel, english pronunsiation) by komitted swuidaid on frustraigun over his faeilyur ty establig xu metrik sistem in U.S. Hi spent e laif taim and ol his muni traiing ty bring it about. Ai fill just as strongli abaut xu establigment ov xu AMERIKAN STANDARD FONETIK ALFABET.

Ernest A. Forssgren

3810 Pleasant Ridge Rd, Annandale 22003 Virginia.

Forssgren's Standard American Phonetic Alphabet.

had all, within a few days, been desecrated by the enemy. On the night of the 2nd the government left for Bordeaux, and General Galliéni ominously promised he would defend Paris 'to the end'. A million people, women, children, the old, the infirm, the rich and the frightened, fled from the doomed city. Proust was both infirm and rich, though no coward; he stuck it out till the 4th, and then left for Cabourg.

Céleste not only agreed to come with him, but jestingly proposed to disguise herself as a man, an offer which he prudently rejected. The train took twenty-two hours instead of the peace-time five, and was crammed with fellow-fugitives. On the way he thought with anguish of Robert at Verdun, of his friends in danger, of poor Agostinelli. Agostinelli! Seven years ago at Cabourg, a young man of nineteen, a Saint Cecilia in his black cape, he had driven his sleepless master through the landscapes of peaceful Normandy; a year ago he had said: "I can't bear to see you looking so sad," and returned to captivity in Paris; and now he had ceased to exist, and his drowned body was corrupting far away into dust. Would not his ghost meet the master who had slain him, at Cabourg? Proust murmured to himself a favourite line of Verlaine: *'Ah! quand refleuriront les roses de septembre?* —When will September's roses flower again?'[1] At the Grand Hôtel he occupied room No. 147; and Céleste, revisiting the spot in 1953, recognised the little circular window at the end of the corridor, to which he would walk every evening in his dressing-gown, and watch the sun sinking below the sea-horizon.

He emerged at last from the Grand Hôtel to visit the hospital of Cabourg, now crowded with hundreds of wounded soldiers from the Marne. To his relief he found that most were only lightly injured: they ate, slept, walked and laughed. He went every day with gifts, fifty packs of playing-cards, sets of draughts, boxes of chocolates. Some of his new friends were coloured troops from Morocco and Senegal. One day he heard a tactless lady visitor greet her patient with: "Good morning, nigger!", to which the outraged black replied: "Me nigger, you old cow!!"; and he used the incident for Odette's anecdote of Mme Blatin viewing the Cinghalese in the Jardin d'Acclimatation.[2]

One day, when Proust was too ill to see them, Mme Greffulhe called with 'a gentleman', whom he learned later to have been Montèsquiou. The Palais Rose had been commandeered by the Army, and the home-

[1] Verlaine, *Sagesse*, III, iii.
[2] I, 536.

Ernest Forssgren, at age sixty-seven, on a visit to Sweden in 1961.
The photo was taken at the Grand Hotel in Stockholm.

off the coast of Ireland. It was the boat I almost decided to take.[91] Nearly all passengers were saved, only a handful of lives lost. Now we all began to feel fearful. There was a great deal of tension and anxiety. When would a torpedo strike? We were only at the halfway mark. The escort had turned back and we were all worried. So far it had been a fairly smooth sea, but the fifth day it got awfully rough and most of the passengers were seasick, including myself. The day passed without incidents and we began to feel safe. If we were going to be torpedoed, it would have happened by now. As I had promised, I started to write a letter to MP, hoping it would reach him. All Atlantic mail was censored by the English, and a lot of it never reached destination. Three more days and we landed safely in New York. Second class did not have to go to Ellis Island. It was an exciting sight to see the Goddess of Liberty, holding the torch lighting the way to freedom. The real excitement came as we approached New York harbor, and saw the amazing skyline. It was like entering some fairyland, all those skyscrapers. It was a stupendous sight, undreamed of. What a great country this must be! The land of

91. Forssgren's memory is playing tricks on him here. He left France for America (via Liverpool) in late March 1915 and arrived in New York on April 6, aboard the *Transylvania*. The *Cymric* was sunk on May 8, 1916, on an eastbound sailing (New York to Liverpool) and therefore could not have been the ship that Forssgren "almost decided to take" on its fateful voyage. As we shall see, Forssgren is also confused about the date of the sinking of the *Lusitania*, which he places in 1917 but which actually occurred on May 7, 1915. This date is a closer match to his sailing to New York, so perhaps it was the next westward sailing of the *Lusitania* that he was considering. But even if one accepts this hypothesis—Liverpool was the *Lusitania*'s home port— the departure date is off by about a month. (The *Transylvania*, destined to be sunk in 1917, was taken over by the British government in May 1915 to be used as a troop ship.) Forssgren maintains that second-class passengers like himself did not have to go through immigration at Ellis Island, but that is where I found the record of his arrival in New York City.

opportunities. The land that had enjoyed freedom for centuries, from its birth.

After the usual custom and emigration formalities, I retrieved my money from the purser and was ready to disembark. I had gotten acquainted with a young man aboard ship who suggested we take a taxi together to the YMCA, not far from the Times Square, where he had stayed before. I got a room to myself for only a dollar a day. Charlie was acquainted with New York and offered to show me the town. It so happened the last day aboard ship a playful gust of wind had lifted my hat from off my head and deposited it in the ocean. It was a darby I had bought in London from a clark, both spelled with an E, so Charlie was going with me to buy a new one and see to it I wasn't going to get gypped. We passed a bank near Broadway and I decided to go in and exchange and deposit my money. I received $210.00 which was according to the current rate; and, deposited an even $200.00. We found a haberdashery shop where I bought a derby from a clerk.

Aboard ship I had made the pleasant discovery that the Americans spoke a far more sensible English than the English. That is why I mixed with the Americans exclusively. In the American language home is pronounced just that way; not 'oume, houme, or even Hume as a "prime ass" might call himself. The English spell jail, gaol, lieutenant, stolen from the French, is utterly erroneously pronounced leftenant. LEF-TENANT—the word "lieutenant" means literally lieu, stead, place, tenant, holding, keeping, and has absolutely nothing to do whatsoever with the LEFT—English "logic" and so on and on ad infinitum.[92] Why the English are always spelling

92. Forssgren is right about the French etymology but wrong, of course, about the British pronunciation being based on a misreading of "lieu" for "left." According to the *Oxford English Dictionary,* the pronunciation is difficult to explain, but may result from the "rare O[ld] F[rench]. form *leuf* for

words one way and pronouncing them another way I'll never know, unless it is to set themselves apart as the "BEST," the "GREATEST" people on earth. They have to have something to distinguish themselves from the "plebians" of the rest of the world. The English [language] in its present state, is foisting such a hardship, NEEDLESSLY, on people who are, unfortunately forced to learn this, "spellingly unpractical" language which has rightfully been called the "bastard language," even by the English themselves.[93] It is made up of words "borrowed" from different foreign European languages and in most cases corrupted beyond recognition. Even the alphabet is mostly a corruption. Not a single vowel is correctly pronounced in the English alphabet. I liken the English language to a musical instrument with every string out of tune.

Since my story has a great deal to do with languages, I feel it would not be too much of a digression to, at this point, touch upon a subject which has been closest to my heart ever since I arrived in America, in the year 1915, namely the spelling reform of the AMERICAN LANGUAGE. It must be conceded by language experts, especially Continental Europeans, that to do anything effective, the AMERICAN language must have an entirely new basis: a revision of the present alphabet, i.e., go back to, insofar as possible, the original pronunciation of the letters of the alphabet, indeed improve upon the use of it. As one of many who have tried to bring about a solution towards a reform in the spelling of the AMER-

---

lieu. . . . It seems likely that the labial glide at the end of the OF. *lieu* as the first element of a compound was sometimes apprehended by Englishmen as a *v* or *f*." Forssgren typed "world" for "word" in this sentence, but the error was corrected by hand.

93. Forssgren's conclusion is surprising, given what he does know. French and all the romance languages, each of which derived from a corruption of Latin, could equally be called "bastard" languages.

ICAN language, I wish herewith to introduce my suggestion for a reformed alphabet which I have named "THE STANDARD AMERICAN PHONETIC ALPHABET." The English themselves have finally come to the realization that something must be done about their obsolete spelling, which is as obsolete as their ridiculous medieval money system and their system of measures; therefore I consider my suggestion for a spelling reform very timely. The "solution" coming out of England (not surprisingly) based on the "Shavian Alphabet," consisting of some 40–48 letters and characters, will, of course, double the existing confusion and chaos and is much too absurd for comment.[94] As I have mentioned, the English alphabet and the language as spoken by the English is a musical instrument with every string out of tune. It has been said that the English have some 30 or more different shades of vowel sounds which they propose to dignify with special letters and characters (and we are supposed to learn them) which most of them are <u>sour notes</u> and should be eliminated, and the rest be brought back in tune.

"THE AMERICAN STANDARD PHONETIC ALPHABET"[95]

As originated and suggested by Ernest A. Forssgren; originally introduced and presented in the year 1917.

For the sake of uniformity, consistency and the fact that in most Continental European languages the Latin E is used mostly as the "consonant vowel" to facilitate the pronunciation of the consonant sound. The word consonant means literally with sounding, with sound. The Latin E is used in conjunction with the "Consonant sound." Another reason why I have cho-

94. The Irish-born writer George Bernard Shaw (1856–1950), who won the Nobel Prize for literature in 1925, proposed a reform of the English language to make it a phonetic language.

95. Forssgren has reversed the position of the adjective "standard" from the title given just above.

sen the Latin E to go with ALL the consonants is, as I have mentioned, for the sake of uniformity, but mostly so the Americans can get used to the perfect pronunciation of the letter with which they seem to have the greatest difficulty in trying to learn foreign languages. It is an established fact that the English have corrupted the pronunciation of ALL the vowels they have "taken" from the Latin and Greek alphabets. The most flagrant case being the corruption of the vowels E and I. It is, therefore, most essential to revert back to the correct pronunciation of these two vowels in order to eradicate the confusion which the wrong pronunciation of these two letters, specifically, create[s]. I need only point out the fact that these letters are pronounced correctly in speech, nine times out of ten or more. Why are they not correctly pronounced singly, as in all other languages, and do away with the misleading confusion?

To make a language 100% phonetic, each letter or symbol can have BUT ONE SINGLE PRONUNCIATION. Thus the consonants are: Be, Ce*, De, Fe, Ge*, He, Je*, Ke, Le, Me, Ne, Pe, Qe*, Re, Se, Te, Ve, We, Xe*, Ze.

Vowels: A, open as in fat, AA closed as in far, AE as in air; E, open as in den, EE closed as in deer*; I as in kin, II long as in keen; O, open as in pot, OO, closed as in poor; U, open as in nut, UU closed as in nude; Y, short as in nook, YY long as in noon, which is the same as in the Russian language. As there are various shades of more or less perceptible vowel pronunciations, it will be necessary to appoint a committee of competent and qualified language experts to decide on a standard pronunciation as regards the vowels. In reciting the alphabet, the vowels should be pronounced by their closed and long sounds. The consonants as I have here suggested <u>cannot be improved on. They are perfect</u>. The letter U is a vowel and therefore has only one sound, as U in rude, and NOT "yew" as according to the <u>English corruption</u>.

Comments: Ce, pronounced as in check, identical with the Italian. Ge*, always hard as in go. Je*, always as in jet. Qe*, as in she; Xe*, as in there. N.B. All letters and dipthongs have ONLY ONE SOUND, in order to make the alphabet 100% PHONETIC. NO NEED TO COMMIT SPELLING TO MEMORY; NO NEED OF A DICTIONARY; NO NEED TO CHANGE TYPEWRITERS. THERE ARE NO DOUBLE CONSONANTS.

To point out the absurdity of the proposed English alphabet with 40 to 48 characters I am comparing it with the world's clearest, most distinct language, namely the Italian, acknowledged by artists in the musical field to be the world's most beautiful language. It has only 23 letters including 5 vowels, with E and O having an open and closed [sound], a total of 7 vowels. Italian, the world's most beautiful language, is without a single sour note. I have said this about the French language and I still stand by it. It is equally as beautiful with elegance added.

Ai trust xat xu riidur ov xis propoosal wil kiip his maind open and lyk at xis sujestiun objektivli. Maeni ieers ago ai broot xis aidea ov xu "Amerikan standard fonetik alfabet" ty xu atenqun ov a profesor in ingliq, an Amerikan. At furst hi wos waildli opoosd ty it. Hauevur, hi promisd ty studi xu proposiqun moor cloosli and wud giv mi his kandid opiniun leitur. Aftur a wiik hi kaem ty sii mi, ful ov enxuusiasm, and begd mi nevur ty giv up. Hi eksakted xis promis from mi a qort taim bifoor hi daid, 16 ieers ago. Hi sed it furniqes a purfekt soluuqun ty xu speling problem.[96]

96. Editor's transcription in "bastard" English: I trust that the reader of this proposal will keep his mind open and look at this suggestion objectively. Many years ago I brought this idea of the "American Standard Phonetic Alphabet" to the attention of a professor in English, an American. At first he was wildly opposed to it. However, he promised to study the proposition more closely and would give me his candid opinion later. After a week he

Getting back to the main subject, I was now faced with the problem of making a living in a new and strange country. Unfortunately, I had never learned a trade, and could see no way but to continue the same line of work I left behind me in Paris. At least it would provide the best opportunity to save money towards my ultimate goal of [entering the] Sorbonne and my return to my beloved France. An overpowering thought came to my mind. If I loved France why did I not stay and fight for her, or at least join the ambulance corps and earn the right to stay in France. It is true I was called back to Sweden to do my military service, but if I was allowed to emigrate to America, there surely could not be any objection to my joining the ambulance corps if I stayed in France. MP did encourage me to go to America, but I wonder if he had not thought more of me if I had joined the ambulance service. He could have been putting me to a test. I had failed him and that is why he was so sad. He was disappointed in me. Come to think of it, his encouragement to leave was mostly for my personal safety which would be typical of MP. It was rather halfhearted. He probably thought I should have made some effort to try and arrange to stay on in Paris indefinitely in which I might have succeeded, as long as Sweden was not in the war as yet. After I left, he probably reasoned, very logically, that if I could go to America, I could surely have stayed where I was. What would be the difference, and his reasoning would have been right. I was, after all, nothing but "un lâche." I had deserted him and the country and the people that had been so kind to me. Deserted in time of need. How could I dare to think I was going back after it was all over. All

---

came to see me, full of enthusiasm, and begged me never to give up. He exacted this promise from me a short time before he died, 16 years ago. He said it furnishes a perfect solution to the spelling problem.

those brave Frenchmen sacrificing their lives, and I should go back to profit by their sacrifices. What right did I have to think I was ever going to enjoy that wonderful country again? It suddenly dawned on me I had been a despicable coward.

I became obsessed with the idea that I had made a terrible mistake, coming to America instead of staying in France and joining the ambulance corps, my original idea, which MP had talked me out of; that is, he suggested I wait until Sweden entered the war. I wrote MP a second letter telling him how sorry I was having deserted him and France, and that I would return as soon as I heard from him and boat passage could be arranged. I gave him the YMCA address as I had given in my first letter, also telling him I would join the ambulance corps immediately upon my arrival in France.[97] As an infirmier or ambulance driver I would not have to kill anyone and would have maybe a 50–50 chance of survival.

It was the day after landing in New York and time to look for a job. I had been told the best place to get work in private service was the Seeley employment agency on West 52nd Street. I had the same luck there as I had when I first arrived in Paris. I was sent to interview a Mrs. V. who lived in a mansion only a few blocks away. She belonged to New York's top 400. By a strange coincidence she knew Prince Orloff and had been entertained in his palace in Paris. She was pleased with my very excellent European references, but remarked how badly I spoke English; so she switched to French which was as bad as my English, as far as the accent was concerned. If I was satisfied to take the position at $50 per month and all "found," I could start the next day, to which I agreed. She rang for her butler, an Englishman, of course, and told me I

---

97. No letters between Forssgren and Proust from this period are known to exist.

was to address him by his surname (Jarvis, not his name) according to English custom. I had been engaged and would he please show me my duties. He was the typical English gentleman's gentleman of impressive appearance. He was my height and yet was able to look down on me, which he did by the simple expedient of tilting his head backwards and looking down his nose. The effect awed me to the point I wanted to address him [as] "your majesty" or at least your highness, but to call him plain Jarvis, I couldn't think of it, at least I couldn't settle for any less than Mr. Jarvis, rules or no. He told me of my duties and finished by saying: "You speak English very badlai," for which compliment I thanked him, but he did not catch on—what Englishman could?

"You must improve quicklai as you will be required to answer the telephoun and receive guests."

He introduced me to the footman who had ushered me in[to] the presence of the lady of the house, a pleasant appearing young man, a Scotsman, and I felt we would get along well. He showed me my room which was very nice, and gave me some pointers about the rules of the house and told me I had to address the butler and ladies' maid by their last names. He showed me the help's dining room which also served as the help's sitting room. He introduced me to the ladies' maid who was having a cup of tea. He had warned me I had to be especially respectful to her. It seems she had been the personal maid of the Duchess of Uppermost, of London and Kent. She was frightfully uppety. I was thinking that something of the Duchess must have rubbed off on to her, a more duchessy lady I had never seen. How could I call her just plain Hairbrush? (which was not her name.) I decided as for the butler and the ladies' maid, it would have to be Mr. Jarvis and Miss Hairbrush. A more ducal pair I never saw. They had their own little dining room, the three of them, Mr.

Jarvis, Miss Hairbrush and Mademoiselle. They could not be expected to eat with the COMMON servants. They were waited on by the kitchen maid the same way as the employers were waited on by the butler and footmen.

The butler gave me a note to take to the family tailor immediately. I was to be measured for a livery, and if I stayed with my employers six months I would get a civilian suit as well. This was indeed a lucky break for me. I had never dreamed I would get a job like that the second day after I landed in America. I could save 30 to 35 dollars a month. In two months I would have the fare back to France. I had made up my mind I was going back as soon as I heard from MP, which I realized might take several months because of the uncertainty of mail.[98]

I was to report the next day at noon. It was the servants' lunch hour.[99] I was introduced to the rest of the staff by the Scotch footman. There was a chef, a Frenchman, the second cook, Swedish. The governess, French, I met later, and we became the best of friends. The footman had jokingly told the chef I was a countryman of his and had just arrived from Paris. It was understandable he was anxious to meet me as he had not been in France for over 20 years as he told me later. He remarked that although I spoke like a Frenchman, I did not look like one. I told him I was Swedish which caused the second cook to prick [up] her ears. I spoke a few words to her in Swedish to which she answered in English which became typical of the rest of the Swedes in the house. More of this later. I became engrossed in conversation with the chef to the point I almost forgot I was engaged to work and was re-

98. Forssgren typed "I had made up by mind."

99. For clarity's sake, I have corrected the position of the apostrophe in Forssgren's "servant's."

minded by the footman who wanted to show me the silver cleaning room. I had told the butler I was one of the "silvermen" at my former position. This would suit fine as the man I was replacing had been the silverman, meaning in charge of the silver cleaning. I was to alternate with William, the other footman, for front hall duty every other day at noon, dressed in livery. I would be off duty every other day after lunch until six o'clock and every other Sunday free if there were no dinner party, which happened seldom on a Sunday, I was told. While I was waiting for my livery to be ready I was to help Gus, the houseman, with his chores. This individual, instead of being friendly as you would expect from a countryman, seemed to have taken a dislike to me. He was curt and surly and would always answer me in English, such as he spoke it, whenever I asked something in Swedish. I don't know why they expected me to speak fluent American after only a few days in the country. It is true, as he observed: "You was ban [have been?] in England and still you speak so bad, your French can't be much better."

So that is it, I said to myself. "Yes, I spent eight months in London, and if I did not learn anything else, at least I learned good grammar, what there is of it. I learned to say you were, not you was."

This was the beginning of a bitter enmity. He would hardly speak to me after that. He had that uncouth Swedish peasant accent that has always been the butt of so many jokes. It was the same with the other two Swedes. It seems they had formed some kind of conspiracy against me, although I had only been in the house a few days. The middle-aged spinster parlormaid would walk away when I started to talk Swedish. It was a mystery to me. With the exception of the two English and the Swedes, I became quite popular with the rest of the help, especially the Irish. I had joked to them about the snootiness of the English butler and maid that treated me so condescendingly. This, of course, endeared me to the Irish. I had asked myself many times what I had against the English. My mind took me back to the last days in London. Had not the lady for whom I had worked as footman, only seven months, given me such a fine reference, and come down to the kitchen the day I left and supervised the fixing of sandwiches and goodies I was to take with me on my journey to Paris? I searched my mind and could find nothing against the English. In fact, I had been treated much better in England than in my native Sweden. The only thing I had against the English was that overbearing arrogance in their speech by the "gentry" and their peers of those days. The language itself was the main thorn in my side: the crazy spelling and the contradictory pronunciation. I could find no excuse for it, comparing it with other European languages. Then with my first encounter with an Englishman in America, there was that abominal condescention . . . the English always screaming at you: "We are better than any people on earth!" And then I might, in this connection, point out the other extreme of the English "language"—that of the common people, the "cockney." There is no language on earth quite so uncouth, utterly without character. Nothing like the charm, warmth, character and even humor of the Irish, Scotch, Welch and the Southern and Western drawl and brogues of the American.

To the credit of the Americans I want to state here that they have done wonders with the "bastard language." They have made it the world's richest, most flexible, versatile and masculine language, lending itself with suppleness to the description of every conceivable situation and condition in the fewest and simplest words and terms possible. In fact, the Americans have created the unique AMERICAN LANGUAGE, which the whole world is trying to copy. Now, let us make it perfect, let us make it 100% PHONETIC. It can be done without disturbing the present printed alphabet. I wish here to appologize to the reader for this seemingly unrelated language digression, and promise to stay on the main theme of this account to the end of same.

Since I had never taken any serious interest in the English language, feeling the way I do about it, and never expecting to have to use it, my vocabulary was, necessarily, very limited, so I cannot be blamed for using my only means of communication, Swedish and French. Swedish was out, as the Swedes would not speak to me in that language, so I was forced to confine myself to the use of French if I wanted to carry on any lengthy conversation. This is why I divided my spare time with the chef and Mademoiselle, the governess. They had learned about the resentment the Swedes held against me, and were puzzled over the reason. I told the chef he should never have said I spoke better French than he. "It is understandable I should, just coming from France, and, as you say, you have hardly ever spoken French in over 20 years. It is the same with those Swedes; they are ashamed of their Swedish, speaking it so badly, and I noticed their 'English' is not much better. The real reason is the typical Swedish jealousy and envy. I can do something they cannot do. Den kungliga svenska avundsjukan.[100] The royal Swedish envy. It is the most prominent Swedish character trait. It is of such eminence that the Swedes themselves have dignified it with this royal title, so it cannot be said that I am biased, as it is too well known for that. Not that it has anything to do with the Swedish royalty. And speaking of royalty, you, Mademoiselle,

100. My friend Bob Borson tells me that this was still a familiar expression in Sweden when he lived there in the 1960s.

who are French, must know something about the present Swedish royal family, the Bernadotte Dynasty. It was founded by the great Marechale [maréchal] under Napoléon premier, Charles Jean-Batiste Bernadotte, Prince de Ponte Corvo [Pontecorvo].[101] It is a young and vigorous dynasty. Their vigor is attested by their extraordinary longevity. They are the world's most admirable, democratic Royal Family. Remarkably talented, especially in the arts; poetry e.g., the most beautiful poem ever written in Swedish, 'Östersjön' (The Baltic)[,] was written by King Oscar II. In music, the young Prince Gustav who composed one of Sweden's most beautiful songs[,] 'In the Fragrance of Roses' (i rosens doft), the beauty of which, both music and lyrics, attest[s] to his musical genius. He also composed Sweden's most popular student song. Had it not been for his unfortunate and untimely demise in his twenties, Sweden might now rate with Norway, Finland and Denmark in music. Then we have Prince Eugene, one of Sweden's greatest painters. I could go on and on, but I don't want to get ahead of my story other than to state that in my humble opinion the Bernadotte Dynasty is the greatest that has appeared on the European scene in the past several centuries."

"What an interesting account! To think one of our countrymen becoming your King, and his Queen, Désirée, a French woman, and what an illustrious royal pair they were according to what I have read," Mademoiselle said. "How fantastic."

"And if my guess is right, and the will and advice of the present King Gustav V is allowed to prevail, Sweden will stay

101. Jean-Baptiste-Jules Bernadotte (1748–1844) became a marshal under Napoléon, was elected crown prince of Sweden in 1810, and later became King Charles XIV John (1818–44).

out of this war. King Gustav is very popular and I feel sure the people will stand behind him in his wish to keep Sweden neutral. He is a great sportsman and quite a humorist and talented like most of the Bernadottes. To illustrate his popularity and humor, there is the anecdote, one of many, about him. Asked by a reporter why he moved about so much without a bodyguard, he is alleged to have said, 'Bodyguard? I have over seven million of them.' Ever since the Bernadottes took over the reins of government, Sweden has never suffered war. Long live the Bernadottes!"

Although I spent most of my spare time with Mademoiselle and the chef, who seemed genuinely fond of me and began to consider me a Frenchman, since I spoke without an accent, the three of us formed the "French clique." I found some time to spend with the Irish, who also had become very friendly. They had become my main American teachers. They liked the idea of my calling it the American language instead of English, and went along with it. I had decided I was not going to be unfair to the English, and was going to think kindly of them, but when the Irish told me how the English had used, abused and misused the Irish, even I got my Irish up. We had regular sessions over a cup of tea, raking the English over the coals, and I must say I enjoyed it. I was right in the first place, after all. I decided I really did dislike the English wholeheartedly.

My job soon became routine, but I was not happy with the undeserved resentment against me on the part of those I just mentioned. I asked myself what was so remarkable about being able to speak French any more so than any other language. What is truly [words missing] and the glamour of the French language is enough to rouse envy and jealousy of anyone who can speak flawlessly, and considering the teacher I had, that is the way I spoke it. This was the reason behind the resentment. It was a very unreasonable attitude, since I was considerate enough to avoid speaking it, except in the company of the French alone.

Being very fond of nature I used to take walks in the nearby Central Park on the afternoons I was off duty. One day I was walking near a rather secluded part of the park when a man came up to me and wanted to sell me a diamond which weighed a carat, he said, and I could have it for fifty dollars. I had seen enough real diamonds in my servant capacity to know it was not real, and if it was, it was bound to be stolen. I told him I resented him thinking I was so dumb I didn't know it was only a piece of glass—what did he take me for. I must have looked awfully green horny [like a greenhorn] to him. Just then an accomplice of his had approached me from the rear and struck me a terrific blow on my head with some blunt instrument which caused me to black out for a few seconds, as I fell over a bench. As I came to, I found my wallet gone and my head was swimming. I was in a daze and headed back to the house and told the other footman what had happened. Mrs. V. was at home, and he told her about the mugging, and was kind enough to suggest I might need a doctor. She sent for one right away. I was still in a daze when the doctor arrived. He examined me and told me it was a slight concussion. My hard derby most likely saved me from a more serious injury. Mrs. V. had sent for the police. I was asked for a description of my assailants, and how much did I lose. I told the police it was only six dollars as I had been warned not to carry much money walking in the park. So I was only out six dollars and a derby. I got away cheap. Two weeks in New York and this had to happen. Two years in France and nothing like that had happened, as much as I used to roam in Bois de Boulogne and Montmartre in the evenings. I must get back to France as soon as possible.

A few days later I learned the family was moving to the summer residence on Long Island, near the Sound. This delighted me as I would be able to do a lot of saltwater swimming like I did at Cabourg.

The summer passed very pleasantly, thanks to the lovely people I worked for and my French and Irish friends, the Irish with their charming brogue and wonderful sense of humor. One thing worried me greatly, however, not hearing from my father and MP. I had arranged forwarding of mail, but never a word. Could it be that the English cold-bloodedly dumped mail overboard, saving time of censoring, as was rumored? September came and still not a word from my father or MP. What could be the reason? Could MP have died? He was always in delicate health. October came and we were moving back to town. I decided I would seek a job away from New York, a city I had gotten to hate. I had received my civilian suit to which I was entitled after six months service. Mrs. V. seemed genuinely sorry when I told her I was not happy in New York and wanted to seek a place in the country, and I was giving her a month's notice. I loved the country even in winter. She told me she knew a place which should suit me perfectly, [with] a very dear friend of hers. But the job would not be available until the first of the year, as the people were in Florida. This magnificient country mansion was located some thirty miles outside of Philadelphia. When full staffed it usually had about 30 servants. Very nice people to work for. "If you will stay here until then, I shall arrange for Mrs. W. to take you on as footman. They keep four footmen in livery. There you alternate 2 and 2 every other day instead of one and one as here."

I told her I thought it was very wonderful of her to be so kind to me, and I would be glad to stay until the first of the year.

"Are you then satisfied with me, Madam?"

"Perfectly, but I am sorry you are leaving my service, for I would have liked you to stay on, but I won't stand in your way."

"Could I ask you another favor, Madam? Would you please not mention about me speaking French, as you have told me Mrs. W. has a few Swedes in her household."

"I think I know what you mean. I can't understand why you don't get along with your own countrymen. I know it is not your fault."

"No stupid ignorant Swede will stand for another Swede speaking the coveted, glamorous French language, especially flawlessly, as Mademoiselle has indicated to the Swedes in your household."

"I must say your English has improved, although you have a slight Irish accent."

"I try to speak American in preference to English and the Irish come closer to doing it. Besides, they have been my principal teachers, the Irish in your household. You, madam, speak American as distinguished from English. Your speech is natural, without the typical English affectation like your butler and maid, yet refined and cultural. <u>American</u> is a language apart from English. In this country there are many versions of it, from the crudest to the most refined, without a slightest touch of English. The reason for that is, the Americans are a people devoid of inhibitions and affectation, a natural, democratic people, a people of common sense, or uncommon sense rather."

"You do dislike the English, Ernest."

"Yes, because I dislike arrogance, affectation and pretense. There is a vulgar term describing their 'elegance.' They are constantly 'screaming' at the whole world how much better they are. They are a lot of conceited silly asses. I despise the English! However, I have met some very fine English people, intelligent people, who have agreed with me 100%, but they did not have these objectionables I have just mentioned in their speech."

It was now getting close to Christmas, 1915. I finally got a letter from my father. He was wondering why he had not heard from me, since the letter I wrote upon landing in the United States. He had written since he first heard from me. He suggested it had something to do with the English censorship. He was hoping Sweden would stay out of the conflict. As I had surmised, the King and the people wanted to stay neutral, but some of the military brass seemed to favor joining with Germany, as I recall. Conditions in Sweden were not too bad, although inflation had set in and things began to be scarce and there was talk of rationing.

It was a great disappointment not to receive word from MP. What could have happened? I had written three times and still no answer. I debated with myself, should I return to France anyway? My letters must have been intercepted or lost somehow. I knew if he were alive he would do anything in his power to contact me, thinking of our parting and our parting words. Either he had died or had not received any of my letters. I decided on writing a fourth letter. Making inquiries about accommodations back to France, I was advised it would be very risky and foolish for anyone already in America. Why would I want to go back at this stage of the war? I thought I had rather strong reasons. However, it would be futile if, after all, MP had died.[102] I will wait until spring and see what would happen.

It was now the first week in January, and true to her promise my lady had talked to Mrs. W., who would be glad to

102. For clarity, I have omitted a period Forssgren typed after "MP."

engage me on her recommendation. I was to report to Mrs. W.'s country place the following Monday. I was to wire and say when I would arrive in Philadelphia, and a chauffeur would meet me at the station. He happened to be French and I had all I could do to keep from giving away the game. I had to laugh when he pointed out that I was speaking English with a mixture of French and Irish accent, and that he had heard I was Swede. I told him I came from the northern province of Sweden, called Lappland, and we spoke a different dialect to the rest of Sweden. I was glad I did not have to lie to him [as I would have] if he had pursued the matter of my French accent. We arrived at the mansion of Mrs. W. I was overwhelmed with the wintry beauty of the place. It was like a fairyland. I knew I would be happy to work here. The chauffeur helped me with my baggage and introduced me to the footman who came to receive me at the back door and took me to my room. The place seemed to be swarming with servants. It was late afternoon and the help were to have their dinner at six o'clock. Henry told me that as soon as I was ready to come down to the staff's mens' [sic] sitting room, a sort of club room, where the liveries were kept, and he was sure he could fit me with a livery right away, as there was [sic] a couple of dozen of them dried, cleaned and looking like new. This house obviously went for tall men. The first one I tried fitted me perfect, and I was all set to take up my duties. I asked Henry if he was American since he spoke like one. No, he was from northern England.

"But you don't have a trace of English accent. I am glad of that."

"Where I come from we don't like that highfalooting Oxford accent."

This was most refreshing, I thought. "I hear there are a few Swedes here."

"There are seven including my wife who does not work in the house. Got enough to do taking care of my kids. You will like her."

"I am sure of that if she is as sensible as you are."

I was introduced to the head butler, also English, but you could hardly tell it by his speech. He seemed very nice and shook hands and wished me welcome to L-hall. He likewise was married to a Swedish woman, not working in the house, but like Henry they lived in cottages like all the married employees in a special section of the estate. H.T., the butler, took me to Mrs. W.'s private sitting room and introduced me to Mrs. W., a very charming and beautiful lady, and much to my surprise [she] offered her hand, wishing me welcome to L-hall, hoping I would like it there. "Mrs. V. has spoken very highly of you and says you are the best silver man she ever had, so you will be in charge of the silver with Henry."

He took me down to the help's dining room seating 24 people, as it was the help's dinnertime. He made a general introduction, saying this is Ernest, another Swede, and seated me next to Bertha, the Swedish parlor maid. I knew right away I was going to like her a lot. I discovered right away she had a terrific sense of humor. Here was one Swede I was going to get along with. For the first time I really felt at home in America. Here I could be happy while waiting for the all-important development, my return to France. I still felt I would eventually hear from MP. The staff consisted of seven different nationalities. There was only one American, Mr. W.'s private barber and masseur. We were four men in livery beside[s] the head butler, two Englishmen and another Swede. It was a rather strange fact that these three Englishmen were the only English in the house, and all were married to Swedish women and, evidently, happily. They were all three American citizens, a very unusual fact for Englishmen. I wondered if their Swedish wives had something to do with that. It is a known fact that the Swedes are quicker in becoming American citizens than any other nationality.

I had not held my position many days before I realized I was faced with a new problem. As the junior footman it was my job to serve lunch to Miss F., the young daughter, and to Mlle. H., the Swiss governess, in what was called the breakfast room, although it was larger than the average dining room in an ordinary home. The main dining room with a seating capacity of 70 people was used for lunch and dinner parties. Breakfast was always served on special trays in the principals' bedrooms. Miss F. and M[lle] H would speak English most of the time, but whan something was said not meant for my ears they would switch to French, although Miss F. was not very good at it and M[lle] H, being Swiss, did not speak Parisian. What to do? It was not fair to listen in on their private conversation. When they switched to French the first time I became the subject of their conversation. Miss F. complimented me on my looks and what she called my aristocratic bearing. I could be one of the European nobility in disguise, escaped from the European war, like so many that were flocking to America these days. Miss F. was saying, "Mother doesn't seem to know much about him other than he is highly recommended by her friend, Mrs. V., and the way she spoke of him you would think he was some kind of a protégé of hers."

"There is a mystery about that man," Mademoiselle said. "I don't like him. I think he is some kind of phony."

All this was, of course, said in French, and I got every word of it. Although I was supposed to stay in the dining room until they had finished their meal, I decided the best thing I could do was to leave the room when they switched to French, usually at the end of the meal. I would pop in at intervals to see if there was something more they wanted. This, curiously enough, had the reverse effect. A few days later, as I cought some snatches of their conversation, I heard M[lle] H say in French, "Do you notice how he resents us talking? He leaves the room as soon as we switch languages."

I don't know why M[lle] H should take such a dislike to me, but she sensed there was something wrong which, in a way, there was, but I was determined to keep my secret, since I realized what it might mean with that bunch of dumb Swedes in the house. It would be the same as at Mrs. V.'s, only worse. With the exception of Bertha, who was very intelligent, they were an unfriendly lot, and always refused to answer in Swedish when I talked to them in that language. It struck me as if the Swedes were ashamed of their own language. It is typical of them, and a well-known fact. I might observe here that the type of Swedes who go for that line of work are far from the intellectual type, and certainly not representatives of Swedes in general. Occasionally you come across someone like Bertha, and, should I say, someone like myself.

Time went on and I was becoming accustomed to all the various conditions pertaining to my job and was getting to like it better and better, as I found my employers wonderful people to work for, especially the young lady, Miss F. She certainly was no snob. She always treated me very friendly. She was somewhat of a tomboy and up to all kinds of practical jokes which she tried to inveigle me on. I will never forget one that almost turned out disastrously in which I was an accomplice, culprit. The upstairs maids used to carry some enormous paper bags in which they would retrieve trash and things from paperbaskets etc. Miss F. had roped me in on a fearful conspiracy, and as she was my boss in a way I had to obey orders. Since all the bombing was going on in Europe, and a war was on, she had decided L-hall was to be bombed. It was to happen while the servants were having their lunch. She the captain and I the corporal. I was to take three or four of those big paper bags and put one inside the other to reenforce them and then fill the reenforced bag with water from the faucet of the maid's cleaning closet up on the fourth floor and tie the top securely and tight. I don't think I have ever handled anything so heavy in my life. It must have been all of 30 or 40 gallons of water. It took all of my strength to carry, but since it was in a good cause I had to exert every ounce of strength. Now I was to carry it to the stairwell and let it drop to the basement where the servants were having their lunch. I was very reluctant but [Miss] F. said, "I take full responsibility, you have nothing to worry about."

Well I dropped the bag from four stories to the basement. As I recall it, the effect was a miniature Hiroshima. The water splashed all the way back up to the fourth floor. The explosion was terrific. The servants rushed from the dining room screaming, "The Germans are bombing."

I don't think I ever heard such a big noise as I had produced. There we stood, Miss F. and I, looking down the stairwell laughing our heads off, the servants running around like scared cattle, not knowing what had happened untill finally one of them heard us laughing and looked up at us, and then everybody started laughing. It was said later it was the biggest joke ever to be pulled off at L-hall. We, Miss F. and I, jointly apologized to Pat and Mike (their real names), the two Irish housemen, who were faced with the cleaning job. Miss F. promised them $5 each. As I walked down to have my lunch I noticed the marble floor in the basement was badly cracked where "the bomb" had landed. It made me worry about subsequent repercussions. But there were none and Miss F. kept her promise, taking all the responsibility. Mr. and Mrs. W.

had a good laugh when they heard about it. Later some stone-masons came to fix the damage.

I had been on the job some weeks when I received another letter from my father, but still no news from MP. The news was about the same as the previous letter. Prices still rising and commodities more and more scarce. It began to look as though Sweden might stay out of the war altogether. My parents were well and everything as usual. Employment had picked up greatly and there was a general air of prosperity all over Sweden. The "blessings" of war. The two young ladies had stopped talking French in my presence. One day there had been unseasonably mild weather, and I had forgot to close the window I had left open for airing. Mademoiselle, who still seemed to be resentful towards me for some reason or other, said to M[iss] F. in French, "I feel a draft, I wish he would close the window." Not thinking what I was doing I went to the window and closed it. "Oh, mon Dieu", almost screamed Mlle H., "do you suppose he understands French?" she said to M[iss] F., in French. Turning to me she asked, "Vous comprenez le français?" The implication was obvious; I perhaps understood a few words here and there. It would be unthinkable that I, a Swede could know French. It infuriated me, especially because of her unreasonable dislike for me.

"Yes," I said, "I not only understand it perfectly, but I speak it even better than you, and try to disprove that."

"Why haven't you said something about it before?"

"Puisque persone me l's demande." [Parce que personne ne me l'a demandé: Because no one asked me.]

"Mais vous l'auriez due nous prevenir." [Mais vous auriez dû nous prévenir: But you should have informed us.]

"It is true, but I had a reason."

She stalked away, furious and red in her face.

"Bravo, Ernest," said Miss F. and laughed. "I suspected it all along. But why did you leave the room as soon as we switched to French?"

"Obviously I had no right to listen in on your private conversation."

"You are not only very smart but also very tactful. My mother is really going to enjoy this. Do you mind if I tell her? She will be very amused. She likes you a lot."

"Thank you, Miss F."

"Mademoiselle has said that sometimes she seemed to detect a slight French accent in your Irish brogue. Why is it you haven't got that typical accent like the rest of the Swedes?"

"Because it is so crude."

"And why the Irish accent?"

"Because the Irish were my first American teachers, and because I wanted to rile the snooty English in my former employment at Mrs. V.'s. As a matter of fact I can imitate almost any accent. You have heard my French, what do you think of it?"[103]

"It is perfect, even better than M[lle] H's French, as you said. But why didn't you let on when you first came? I should think you would be proud, especially the way you speak it. You are very modest."

"There is a reason which you will soon know."

Miss F. was a very intelligent 16 year old girl. "From now on we must speak [French]. I want to learn your beautiful pronunciation. Mlle H is Swiss and does not speak Parisian like you do. Mother will be speaking French with you from now on. She loves France, the French people and the lan-

103. This question is another indication, in spite of Forssgren's pride and boasts, that he is in many ways naïve about languages: he is asking an American who speaks beginner's French to judge the quality of his accent.

guage. But for the war we would be there now. We have spent many winters on the Riviera."

The cat was out of the bag. The news had gotten around. If Ernest speaks as good French why did he want to keep it a secret? His French can't be very good, the Swedes had decided, or he would be talking it all the time. His French is so poor he is ashamed to talk it, that is why. That was the verdict of the Swedes as expected, anything said to the contrary not withstanding. That was the report I got from good old Bertha. I had to promise to teach her some French. She had as much admiration for it as I did. I was on duty in the front hall with the other Swedish footman. "You speaking French like a Frenchman, my foot." I wasn't going to argue with the ignoramus. I just ignored him. Mrs. W. was coming down the stairs and headed straight for me speaking French like a Frenchwoman to know all about it. She had been so curious about me keeping my French a secret, so she had called her friend Mrs. V. who had explained everything, and told me she understood and did not blame me, but hoped it would not come to the same situation here. I told her I had already felt the first impact. She was telling me they were giving French plays in Philadelphia every month and would be glad to have me accompany them. "You speak French remarkably well, I must say."

"If you knew who I had for my teacher, you would understand, Madam."

"You must tell me all about yourself. I shall be interested to hear about it later."

What strange people, these rich Americans, so democratic; they treat you almost like an equal. So natural, without the condescention of the English. It was the same with Mrs. V.

The two French maids were delighted to learn I was a Frenchman[,] as they put it, and from then on we never spoke anything but French, the same as with my employers. The

Swiss governess ignored me completely. She had arranged to have the other Swede serve the meals for her and Miss F. so now they could go on talking French at table to their heart's content. I had insulted her grievously. Bertha was delighted with the turn of events. The rest of the Swedes showed their resentment, just as I thought, just as at Mrs. V.'s. Bertha agreed with me: "the ROYAL SWEDISH ENVY." What on earth else could it be, since I had made every effort to be friendly[?] All the rest of the staff were very friendly and congratulated me on my linguistic ability. The Englishmen were especially nice, but the Swede footman I began to think I would have to watch out for. I was talking to the German kitchen maid one day, as I have just a smattering of that language. He had made a play for her but evidently had been given the cold shoulder. She seemed to favor me.

One afternoon I was sitting in the help's dining room having just finished lunch, talking with the two French maids. All had left but the Swede footman. He got up and as he passed behind me he hit me on my right ear such a hard blow that I almost fainted. My ear started to bleed as I got up to run after him, but I could not find the coward, or I would have given him two for one if I had caught up with him. It was his afternoon off as well as mine and I had made up my mind I was going to find him, and I was NOT going to turn the other cheek. I had to get up to my room as my ear was bleeding as well as my nose, and I felt a funny buzzing. In the meanwhile the two maids had rushed to Mrs. W. and told her what had happened. She sent for me and told me she would have her chauffeur take me to an ear doctor in Philadelphia. She would call and make an appointment. She would let her maid know and she would tell me when to be at the doctors [sic] and would I get ready to leave as soon as possible. I thanked her very cordially, as she asked me to report to her as soon as

I got back. The chauffeur would wait while I was at the doctor's. While I was gone she was going to make an investigation to get to the bottom of the whole thing. The maids had told her what they had seen, but did not know what lay behind the incident.

The doctor examined me very thoroughly and found the eardrum bursted and thought the inner ear might be damaged. We would have to see what time would tell. I asked about the ear buzzing and he said it might disappear after a while, but he could see it was a very severe blow I had received. It might even mean permanent damage. He would make the best report on what he had so far and phone Mrs. W. as she requested. If it got any worse I would see him in two days, otherwise in a week, for which he made an appointment. To the chauffeur I had spoken in French, and he was astounded and wanted to know why I hadn't spoken French, the first time when he brought me from the station when I started the job. To prevent what happened today, was my enigmatic answer. I said I would explain some other time.

"I hear you play the violin" [he said].

"Very badly in my estimation."[104]

"You must come and hear my daughter Lea. She is very good and sometimes plays solos in church."

I would be delighted to meet his family and thanked him for the invitation.

Upon my return from the doctor I was surprised to find a policeman waiting for me in the men's clubroom. He invited me to sit down and tell him all about it. What led to the assault. I told him truthfully I could think of no reason other

---

104. This is all that Forssgren tells us about playing the violin. We do know that he owned one since, many years later, he gave it to Marilyn Gordon's family.

than jealousy. He [the Swede footman] overheard me talking German ([of] which I have a faint smattering) to the German kitchen maid, who seemed to favor me, and who previously had given Al, the Swede footman, the cold shoulder. There can be no other reason, as I am very easy to get along with.

"Yes, Mrs. W. tells me you are quite popular with the help except your own nationality, and you seem to be very popular with your employers. I am told you speak perfect French, isn't that unusual for a Swede?"

"Not at all. French and all the Latin languages are much easier to Scandinavians. A Norwegian for instance, you can hardly tell from a Frenchman, after a year or so in France, as far as Language is concerned. English is much harder to me."

"You seem to have mastered it pretty well. But tell me how is it you seem to speak English with a slight Irish brogue? I am very fond of the Irish for their straightforwardness, humor and honesty."[105]

"I prefer their version of the American language, which I call it, rather than the 'real' English."

"Since I am an Irish cop myself, I appreciate what you have just told me, and thank you for complimenting the Irish. I assure you when you have an Irishman for a friend, you have a real friend indeed."

"So I take it you are my friend and I thank you very much."

"I want to talk to the German maid and see what she has to say. We will have to have her testimony, when you prefer charges for assault and battery."

"I don't think I want to do that," I told him.

"When I get all the data there may be charges against this man which the judge will decide for himself."

---

105. This sentence appears to belong to Forssgren, but he has placed it within the quotes for the policeman, who is, we are about to learn, Irish.

There was no uncertainty about the kitchen maid's feelings. "I won't wipe my feet on that skunk," she told the officer. "I hope he gets a year in jail for what he did to that fine fellow, Ernest."

I reported to Mrs. W. who was in her private sitting room. She asked me to sit down as she told me what the doctor had said. It was difficult to determine yet the extent of damage to my ear, but it could very well mean a gradual reduction of hearing, or even a total loss of hearing in that ear. There was a definite damage to the inner ear, but a chance it may heal up over a period of time.[106]

"I sent for the police as soon as I got the doctor's report," Mrs. W. told me. I suppose you have talked to him, as it is up to you to prefer charges against the scoundrel. I have instructed the police to take him to his room as soon as he gets back and see that he packs his things as soon as possible, and keep an eye on him until he is out of the house. I have left a check for a full month's wages with the police who will take him to the police station. You must file charges. He may have to serve a few months in prison which he deserves."

"I don't think I want to do that, Madam. There is a higher power that takes care of matters like that, in due time."

"That is a very lofty attitude for you to take, and maybe you are right."

The officer told me I had a good case and the man could be sent to jail for some time, but I would have to sign a complaint. I told him I did not want to be involved any further, I was satisfied he was fired, and that I won't have to see the rotter again. "I assure you that if he had not run away, and I had caught him at the time, you would have a homicide on your

---

106. Those who knew Forssgren in his later life say that, like many senior citizens, he was hard of hearing but did not wear a hearing aid.

hands. I could never have controlled my anger. So with that in mind, I consider the score evened up."

It was getting dark and towards the help's dinnertime. The rat came sneaking to the back entrance, obviously scared as a mouse and almost fainted when he saw the police who took him to his room and ordered him to pack his things fast, while the officer was watching, and the police would take him to a rooming house or hotel in Philadelphia and [he] should be glad he did not have to stay in jail for sometime, as he would if I had not been kind enough to refuse to sign a complaint against him. The damage to my ear may cause me to lose the use of it. He was lucky getting away so easy. He was given his check and taken from the house, and was not even allowed to have his supper, which was just as well, as he would have been greeted with hostility from the rest of the help, who were full of sympathy for me when they heard of the dastardly act.

It was decided I would continue serving Miss F and Mademoiselle like I did at the start. Miss H, having been told my reason for leaving the room when they switch[ed] to French, and had everything explained, had thought I had been very tactful, and offered her hand in friendship and apology. She was very sorry she had misjudged me. As it was close to the time for leaving for Newport, Rhode Island[,] where the family were to spend the summer, the fired man was not replaced. The Newport house was too small to accommodate any more than about half the staff, the other half would remain at L-hall.

At Newport the life became rather exciting. Mrs. W. was giving a lot of dinners and there were all sorts of entertainments, Newport being the most important summer resort of the prominent 400. We, the servants, would go swimming every afternoon, which was reserve[d] for us, the mornings being reserve[d] for the gentry. We happened to be living a stone's throw from Bailey's Beach which was very handy as we could walk there in our bathing suits. Those days you were half dressed when bathing publicly. The summer was over in no time, and our next move was to Florida.

It was the end of October, 1916, a year and a half since I had left Paris, and still not a word from MP. It could only mean he was dead. With his wealth he would have spared no expense to reach me if he were alive. Our parting scene came back to me very vividly. "Ernest, you must come back and fulfill your ambition, your career. You have talent, even genius, you must not let them go to waste. With my help you shall realize your goal. You need me as much as I need you. We complement each other. So you see you must come back."

But why leave at all? Why leave him in the lurch? Why did I not take a chance with the rest of the French? Why did I leave France, a country I professed to love, its language, its culture? I had been a coward, un lâche [a coward]! I was seized with an indescribable feeling of sadness, of guilt and frustration, and it was all my own fault. Perhaps MP was still alive and had decided to disown me for my cowardice. If so it was well deserved. I had lost my best and ONLY REAL FRIEND, any chance of language or literary career hopelessly gone.[107] I became reconciled to the dreary fate ahead of me.

I decided I was not going to follow a servant career any longer. I was going to quit here and now for good. I told the butler I was not going along to Florida, and had decided I was going to take up some other work. There was no future in private service for me. I had higher ambition. Mrs. W. was very

107. It seems not to have occurred to Forssgren that reading and writing are usually solitary occupations and the best way to undertake a literary apprenticeship.

sorry to hear about my decision but did not blame me. If I ever should change my mind, and things did not turn out as expected, I would always be welcome back and there would always be a place for me. "We will always be glad to have you back." I wrote to my dear friend, Bertha, at L-hall and told about my decision, and asked her to convey my best regards to everybody.

I had been told that a tall slender man like me who could serve as a clothing model could easily get a job as salesman in a man's store. I went to New York with that in mind, in spite of my dislike for New York. After trying several different stores I got a job the second day (seems I get jobs the second day wherever I go) in a first class men's store on 5th Avenue. I had shown my very good references and explained I did not want to follow a domestic career and had only taken that kind of work until I would have a good command of the language, which was understandable, they thought. As I had to look my best they suggested I select a suit from their stock which I could have at wholesale price on credit if I wanted, but I told them I needed a suit anyway and preferred to pay cash. I was to get $20 a week and a small percent on my sales. I got a room at the YMCA, walking distance from the store[,] for only $2.50 a week. If I was lucky with my commissions I thought I might be able to save as much as in private service. I knew I was going to miss the wonderful food you get in private service. However, I discovered I could get a fine meal at Drakes on 42nd Street for only 35 cents, as I recall. I could actually live well on $10 a week board and room. I had every reason to be pleased with things, but my mind was constantly in turmoil. I could not concentrate on my work or anything. My boss even noticed something wrong, and commented on it. I told him it had to do with the continued war. I had dear ones in Paris that I had not heard from in a long time. He was very sympathetic. My mind was continually plagued with doubt, sorrow and grief. I tried to shake it off but it was futile. There was never a moment's rest for my sick mind. I had hopelessly messed up my whole future. My self-recrimination became almost unbearable. Every day I was going through a mental hell.

I was terribly lonely in the big city of New York which I never liked. I was missing my friends I had made at L-hall. The chauffeur's family who seemed so fond of me, and their daughter Lea who played the violin so beautifully, and liked playing duets with me in spite of my musical inferiority. Yes, I missed L-hall. I decided to write H.T., the butler[,] and ask if they would take me back when they opened L-hall in January. It wasn't long until I got a letter telling me I would be most welcome and to let him know when I would arrive, any day after the first, and the chauffeur would pick me up at the station. This news made me very happy. I had come to realize I could only be happy in the country, and from now on it would only be the country for me. There is something terrifying about a city like New York. I never ever wanted to live there again.

I was installed in my room at L-hall, and had visited Lea and her family, played some duets and had a very good time. Everybody had welcomed me back, with some slight exception[,] and made me feel at home. I had even gotten a nice welcome hug from friend Bertha. The family was to arrive the next day and I was wondering what they would think of me, having come back like a prodigal son. I was all curiosity. The following afternoon H.T. and I were in the front hall expecting the family any minute. Suddenly there was the familiar horn blast of the Pierce-Arrow announcing their arrival. We rushed out on the portico and went to each side of the car to help the ladies out. There were Mrs. W., Miss F. and Miss H.

and the two ladies' maids. I was greeted with a warm hand-shake and a welcome from all the ladies, the butler[,] having seen them only a few days previously[,] busied himself with the small pieces of hand baggage.

"How is your ear, Ernest?" Mrs. W. asked.

"Thank you, Madam, it seems alright but for an incessant buzzing, and I don't seem to hear so good with it."

"I want you to go to the ear doctor tomorrow for a check-up. The chauffeur will take you and I shall make an appointment right away."

"Madam, you are so kind, thank you very much. Your concern touches me deeply."

L-hall became alive with activity. There were many parties and dinners planned and a great many house guests, so there was plenty to do. Another footman was added, an Irishman. It was known the Irish were my favorite nationality and I was wondering if it had something to do with it. I was taken by the chauffeur for my ear doctor appointment. The doctor's findings saddened me greatly. My hearing in my right ear [had] lessened considerably. And I might lose the hearing altogether in that ear. Even my left ear was slightly affected. There was nothing that could be done. An operation might help but it would be too risky. This news depressed me greatly. The doctor conveyed his diagnosis to Mrs. W. who expressed much sympathy and thought the scoundrel who did it to me should have been punished.

"He will be," I said. "The law of cause and effect is infalli-ble."

"I do hope it is not quite as serious as the doctor says; doctors have been known to make mistakes."

I was back in my old routine serving the two young ladies, but mostly we had house guests for lunch. Because of this, dinner was always served in the main dining room. There was a great deal of entertainments, much more than the previous winter, with the result that we did not have as much time off as previously. Things went on routinely for the next several months, and then it happened. The <u>Lusitania</u> was sunk with loss of American lives and there followed a series of "may I note" from President Wilson to the Kaiser, and finally America was in it.[108] I decided that I would join the American ambulance corps. In my depressed state of mind I thought I might as well be in and take a chance with the rest. If I had only heard from MP I would not hesitate a minute. Sweden was still neutral and it was said there was very little chance she would be in the war, at least not on the side of Germany. I went to the recruiting post in Philadelphia and announced I wanted to join the ambulance corps. I was given a date for my physical examination for the following week. I told Mrs. W. of my plans, but she thought I should stay out of it as long as Sweden was not in the war. She would be sorry to lose me a second time. If Sweden was in it, it would be different. I went to town for my physical examination and explained [that] although I was of a neutral country I might be willing to join the corps in the near future. I wanted to know if I was able to pass physically. I explained about my ear trouble. They found I had a busted ear drum and impaired hearing and for the present they could not take me, maybe in the future. And that was that. I was not at all cheered by the news but it was what I had feared.

With the war declaration things changed greatly at L-hall. There were fewer parties and all the house guests had left. Mrs. W. went in for red cross activities and the house was set

108. According to Forssgren's chronology, we are now in January 1917, but as mentioned earlier, the *Lusitania* was sunk on May 7, 1915. His chronology is correct regarding the United States' entry into the war: April 2, 1917.

up for red cross work, for making of bandages and such. The time went on and I became ever more restless. The idea of continuing as a domestic servant became abhorrent to me. I decided to quit domestic work for good. I knew I had creative ability and wanted to do creative work. True, my talent lay in the linguistic field, but there was nothing I could do in that direction now. I would have to go to Paris for that, and per- haps yet someday I might realize that ambition. At the pres- ent time things looked hopeless. I gave a month's notice and did not have to feel too badly about leaving as there was some talk about reducing the staff because of the war. Life was to be more austere, even for the millionaires.

I had one time thought I would be interested in machin- ery as it might furnish opportunity for an inventive mind like mine.[109] My leave-taking from L-hall was rather sad. I had made many good friends, but such is life, it must go on . . . Mrs. W. was especially kind and wished me luck and Miss F. was almost tearful. M[lle] H was very cordial. Mr. W. had said good-bye that morning before he left for his office. I felt tear- ful myself, everybody, with very few exceptions, seemed to be sincerely sorry to see me go. I had a touchy [touching?] farewell with Bertha and I promised I would write. Bidding farewell [to] Lea and her family was also very sad, and as someone has said, "Parting is such sweet sorrow."[110]

I looked for machine shops in Philadelphia and surround- ings. I finally landed a job in Camden, New Jersey, as an ap- prentice. After a few weeks on this new job I could see there was room for some improvements that would make for better efficiency and economy. I made a written suggestion to my

109. Forssgren typed "as I might."

110. Is it ignorance or Anglophobia that makes it impossible for Forss- gren to recognize Shakespeare's *Romeo and Juliet* as the source of this quo- tation? Forssgren began this sentence "Bidding farewell with."

immediate boss who in turn took it up with the general manager. My idea was studied and was found to have merit. It was decided to follow up my suggestion and in a short time [it] proved to be so satisfactory that I was given a bonus of $500 and a substantial increase in wages. As I found out later my idea meant thousands of dollars in saving[s] yearly. It was not long after, I became restless and wanted to move on to something better. I hated the grime of the factory, the noise and the hidious surroundings as compared to what I had been used to. My greatest passion had always been beauty, appealing to the eye and ear. I had the greatest love of nature and flowers so I decided to become a gardener's apprentice. I found such a job on one of the millionaire's [*sic*] estates in New Jersey. At last I thought I had found myself in my right element. For the first time I really began to enjoy my work. I was clipping the hedge one day near the patio where the nurse-governess was teaching the 4 year old girl, the daughter of the house, English spelling from a primer with pictures of animals, cat, dog, etc.

"Now, Doris, what does C-A-T spell?"[111]

"Sate," the little girl said—from the mouth of babes . . .

"No, it spells katt," Miss M. said.

"No it don't either," the little girl insisted.

"We will go on. What does D-O-G spell?"

"Dodge," the girl said.

"No, it spells dog, dogg," said Mademoiselle.

111. According to Marilyn Gordon, Forssgren's stint as a gardener's apprentice was on the 2,700-acre estate of J. B. Duke, the tobacco magnate, who raised his only daughter, Doris, there. Doris Duke was born in 1912. The name and the date fit as does the location of Hillsborough, New Jersey. Today the estate is the Duke Farms Foundation. The archives are still in the process of being inventoried and catalogued and may one day yield proof that Forssgren worked there.

"No it don't . . ."

"You must not say don't, doesn't is right . . ."

"Don't is prettier . . ."

Since I was working so close by I couldn't escape hearing this little controversy, and as it had to do with the subject which had always been a thorn in my side, I could not contain myself. I walked up and excused myself for interrupting, and said to little Doris, "You are a smart little girl, you are absolutely right, the book is wrong and so is Mademoiselle. When you grow up you are going to be a very rich lady, and you are going to help change this idiotic spelling and make a big name for yourself, you promise?"

"Yes, I promise. I don't like English. When I grow up I am going to talk only French. I like French, it is nicer than English."

"That's a good girl."

"I like you," she said. Mademoiselle who was Luxembourgeoise could do nothing but laugh.[112] She had as much contempt for the English language as I had. She was surprised when I started talking French to her and we became good friends. I told her how I happened to come to America from France during the war. I had gone there before the war to study the French language. We dwelt for a few minutes on the absurdity of the English language, the way words [are] spelled without rhyme or reason. This is, of course, my own assumption and personal opinion. This is not any reflection against the AMERICAN language of which I have already expressed my idea. I want to express here my admiration for the French-Canadians for not allowing the vile English to be

112. Luxembourgeoise is French for Luxemburger, a native of the small country of Luxembourg, whose southern frontier borders France. Although the country's official language is Luxemburgish, many Luxemburgers speak French as a second language.

foisted upon them. I take my hat off to them. It is a pity that French is not the language of the United States as it might have been.

When I first tried to introduce my PHONETIC AMERICAN AL-PHABET way back in 1917, I was thinking mostly of emigrants entering the United States, who were more or less illiterate, and how much easier it would be for them to learn <u>American</u> with a phonetic alphabet, since their own language was phonetic or nearly so. The confusing English spelling caused many, perhaps the majority, to refuse to learn the English, and decided [*sic*] to stick to their own language. I know this for a fact by personal observation. I thought it could at least serve as an auxiliary alphabet until such time that the student could learn to recognize the "conventional" spelling in reading books and newspapers. I don't know about the blind or deaf-mutes, but I understand they use some phonetic system; it would be a pity otherwise. I can't see a deaf-mute going through the motions of spelling "thorough," "rough," and all the rest of the idiotic "ough's." It's a laugh. The phonetic alphabet will save at least 20 to 25% work for the stenographer and the typist.

Encouraged by my successful suggestion in the machine factory, I began to think of inventions. On my spare time from gardening I would get an idea for an invention and would work on it if I thought the idea had promise. I informed myself on how to go about seeking a patent. It was suggested I make drawings of the article and make out a "claim," then send it to the patent office in Washington and have a search made, which would cost $15. If the idea was patentable it could cost $1000 or more to get a patent. This gives the reader an idea what a struggling inventor has to go through, the disappointments and frustrations; I thought, for instance, I had hit upon a very practical men's garter. I drew a sketch of it and since I was not too far from Washington I decided to conduct my own search. I was amazed at the enormous library of patent books and records. I looked up garters (men's) and could not believe my eyes. There were over 2000 pairs of them patented—how could that be possible?—and if they were laid out next to each other in a chronological order, you could hardly tell the difference one from the other. They must have represented two million dollars or more in wasted money. There is nothing so futile and frustrating as the lot of the inventor. It has been established that 96% of the ideas and inventions submitted for patent have already been patented. So, dear reader, if you get an idea for a patent, don't get excited. There are only four out of a hundred chances you can get a patent, and if you should, the chances of success financially is [sic] practically nil. At this point of my story it is late fall, 1917. If you care to follow me through I will meet you in May, 1922, and we will continue from there.

I shall draw an appropriately black veil over the ensuing five dark years. Years of struggle, disappointments and frustrations, interspersed with occasional encouragements and rising hopes and visions of success, only to be mercilessly dashed against the cruel wall of failure. The inventor is like the gambler: he will keep on throwing good money after bad money, while he has any money left. The law of averages will eventually let him win, even if it is a "long shot." Thus I had experimented with various ideas that looked hopeful, and so my savings went for making models, drawings, claims and searches, etc. I had submitted 32 different inventions and ideas, nearly all of them already patented (nothing new under the sun), but I refused to give up as long as I had a little money. I knew eventually I would make a strike. The war was over, and I was broke. My parents pleaded with me to come home. The only way I could do that was to swim, but I thought it was too far, although I am a good swimmer. I had written I would not go back to Sweden a complete failure. I would continue struggling until I had it made. I was still young and had the greatest capital of all at my command, my health, although my hearing was beginning to fail me.

Came May, 1922, at last a break. Now I had an idea that would pay off, even if not in a spectacular way. My boss was very enthusiastic. He had an acquaintance, a toy manufacturer, who he felt would be interested in my invention, in as much as he was already equipped to make the article without going to the expense of providing special machinery. He made an appointment for me and I went to see him the next day and demonstrated the article. He was immediately interested and wanted to know what I wanted for the idea. I had showed my search and could prove I could get a patent on it. I asked him to make me an offer since I had no idea what it would be worth. He would think it over and make me a cash offer in a couple of days. I asked my employer what he thought I should accept for it. He said it ought to be worth $100,000 if it was worth a cent. I suggested that he exaggerated; it could not be worth that much. We finally agreed that $25,000 would be a fair price, and I should hold out for that. When I saw Mr. G. again he made me a cash offer of $10,000, take it or leave it. I told him I thought it should be worth a whole lot more than that. Wouldn't he make a better offer, one doesn't usually accept the first offer. I said I would make a counter offer, after thinking it over a couple of days. I reported to Mr. L. who had sort of appointed himself as my agent. I told him of the $10,000 offer which he thought was ridiculous. We discussed the matter at some length and decided I was to hold out for $25,000. I went to see Mr. G. the following day and gave him my counter offer. He said, "I'll tell you what I'll do. I will buy a six month's option for $2500 and the rest in six months." I told him I would make a deal if he raised the option money to $5000. It was now I needed the money most urgently. All right, I will pay you $5000 now if you make the total price $20,000, the balance of $15,000 in six months. I told him I would make the deal. And so the contract was drawn up. I got my $5000 check and was gloating, thinking it just about represented what I had lost. I got my money back and in six months I would be practically a rich man. Paris here I come!! My language career cinched although I had lost a lot of time. I was really happy for the first time since I arrived in the United States. Mr. L., my employer, bawled me out. "You are an idiot, you are no businessman, never will be. Why didn't you let me handle it? I don't want you to think I wanted anything out of it for myself, but I wanted a fair deal for you."

"I am sorry, boss, I know you meant the best for me."

"Well, let's forget it, my boy, you have your five grand and that will reimburse your losses. Maybe it's just as well you took the deal as you did."

I wrote my father I would arrive in Sweden on the HMS Gripsholm the last week in June, the earliest accommodation I could get. I was very happy and excited when the time for departure came. I had not seen my parents, brothers and sisters in 10 years. As I was coming back [to the States,] I stored most of my things and was traveling light. I looked forward with great anticipation. I was not coming home broke . . . I had almost $5000 in the bank and was even bringing presents for my family. The world looked rosy. If only that ear didn't keep buzzing like that. The sea voyage was wonderful, fine weather all the way. I wasn't seasick a day. I made some shipboard friends and had a great time. Immediately upon landing I took the earliest train for Norrland for a visit with my parents.[113] It was a wonderful experience after ten long years. I thought my parents had aged greatly, but they were very happy to see their wandering son back. We discussed what I was going to do in the future. I had told them about the windfall, falling in the fall. I was going back to Paris and I was going to become a professor in the Latin languages, even if it is a little late. They were very happy about my presents. After visiting with my parents for a few weeks, I went to visit my sisters and brothers and some other relatives. Time passed quickly, almost as quickly as my money. I have always been the one to pay my way. It is a matter of pride with me. And when you come as a "guest" such a long way, you would think that things would at least be on [a] somewhat recipro-cal basis . . . Well, I found myself strictly a paying "guest." By the time I got back to Stockholm, about two weeks before my scheduled return to America, I was forced to wire my bank in New York for money.

I had been invited to come and spend a few days at my oldest brother's place, which unfortunately I reluctantly ac-cepted. I would have been better off economically and com-fortably in a hotel. I was walking along one of the main streets in Stockholm when I happened to look in a window of a book-shop and saw the name Marcel Proust, literature[']s "dernier cri."[114] Some of his translations were displayed. I became greatly excited and went in to ask the manager if Marcel Proust was still alive. "Why, yes," he answered in surprise. I told him I had been living in the United States for many years

113. Norrland is the northern part of Sweden, comprising a number of provinces.

114. I know of no incident of Proust's contemporaries referring to him, or to any other writer as the "dernier cri," an expression used for the latest fashion or fad.

where he was not yet known. "Yes, he is very much alive and has become a great celebrity. 'Le dernier cri,' as the French call him and his works. He has won the coveted Prix de concours and will probably win the next vacancy in the ACADÉMIE FRANÇAISE."[115] This was a most astounding revelation. It put me in a daze.

I started to debate with myself [if] I should return by way of Paris and visit him, or would I be too presumptious, now that he has become a great celebrity.[116] I decided I would try and visit him. It could not do any harm. Then perhaps a lot of things can be cleared up. I decided to take the train for Paris the next day. As I was not far from the N.M., travel agency, I made arrangements to take the Paris express, leaving early in the morning, and tried to get a sleeper. I wired the Cunard line I would board the ship at Cherbourg instead of South Hampton. Continental European passengers were usually picked up there.

I returned to my brother's place in suburban Orby. Right away he noticed I was in a state of great excitement. I asked

115. The Prix Goncourt, France's most prestigious literary award, is named after the Goncourt brothers Jules and Edmond, whose will endowed it. Although the brothers wrote successful plays and novels, they are chiefly remembered for their famous *Journal* (diary), which covers the years 1851–96. A "prix de concours" is merely a prize won in a competitive scholastic exam. The Académie Française is the famous institute that is charged primarily with overseeing literary and linguistic matters relating to the French language. Although Proust made overtures to writers such as Henri de Régnier and Maurice Barrès to support his nomination to the Académie Française, he did not succeed.

116. Another contradiction, which, when added to what Forssgren is about to say regarding his boarding the ship in Southampton, would seem to indicate that Paris was not even on his itinerary for the trip. This also casts doubt on his claim to have suffered all these years for having abandoned Proust and France.

Forssgren typed "with myself it."

him if he knew MP was still alive. "Everybody knows that. He is talked about a great deal and is very famous."

["]You know that and didn't let me know? Don't you remember MP was interested in my language career, because he realized I had talents for languages. He was going to 'lancer' [launch] me as we say in French, and help me through Sorbonne. I was his protégé."[117]

"Sometime after you left I received a letter from him with a gold louis in it and [Proust] asked for your address in the United States."[118]

"And this you have the nerve to tell me now. Why didn't you give him my address? I had written four letters but evidently someone was intercepting them."

"Well, at that time I did not think you ought to have anything to do with him."[119]

"What did you do with the gold louis, keep it? It would be like you."

"Well, what could I do? I couldn't return it without giving your address. I was doing what I thought best for you."

"A likely story."

"I thought he would think the letter had been stolen, as anyone could feel it contained a coin."

"Stolen is right. Of all the rotters I have encountered, you

117. Forssgren was in Proust's service too briefly to have been considered his protégé.

118. Proust knew Prince Orloff and had many friends in various embassies, including his close friend Antoine Bibesco, posted at the Romanian Embassy in Washington, D.C., during the war years. It would presumably have been fairly easy for him to trace Forssgren had he wished to do so.

119. Marilyn Gordon's family knew that Forssgren was homosexual, although this was not a subject of discussion among them. Did Forssgren's brother know that Forssgren and Proust were homosexual? Since Forssgren does not tell us why his brother thought he should avoid Proust, this dialogue seems rather peculiar.

are positively the lowest. I could kill you, but I don't want to soil my hands."

If it had not been for the presence of his wife, I think I would have thrashed him within an inch of his life.

"You rat, you were always jealous of me. I was very popular with the French and you hated me because of it. You hated me for the pet name 'le Parisien' they gave me, because I was a Parisian like them. I had it on you in every way. You were going to stop me from a linguist career. But for you I could now be halfway to [a] professorship. You may have even conspired with Céleste to intercept my letters, giving her some cock and bull story winning her over to your scheme. God knows Madame Céleste was incapable of any wrong doing.[120] Remember this, you are the most unspeakable scoundrel I have ever known. I shall HATE you more than any other creature as long as I live."

I was able to get all this over to him holding him down in an easy chair with my left hand ready to knock him out with my right if he as much as let out a peep. He had accomplished his purpose. Up to now, he had destroyed my career, my life ambition. Oh, Jealousy, what crimes thou hast committed! My ear was buzzing worse than ever before. I asked my sister-in-law to call a taxi while I packed my things. I pressed a "present" into her hand as I bade her good-bye and said, "This is for you <u>only</u>." The taxi took me to a hotel. The next morning I was on my way to Paris.[121]

I arrived in Paris the following morning after a very interesting journey.[122] As I had been lucky in obtaining a sleeper I

120. This sentence seems to indicate that Forssgren caught the inconsistency in his representation of his relationship with Céleste.

121. The excerpts published in French resume after this paragraph. The editors give the following section the title "Une Visite (Paris, 1922)."

122. The French translator added the phrase "Après plus d'un jour entier de train" [After more than an entire day's train ride].

was well and rested up. I took a taxi to a small hotel where I had stayed before, (the Riviera), near the Grands Boulevards.[123] My intention was to write MP for an interview, so I walked to the address where he lived when I left Paris in 1915. I found the building had been transformed into a commercial establishment.[124] No one knew his address. I knew it would be useless to look in the phone book or le bottin de Paris [telephone directory] as he always kept his address secret.[125] I went to his brother's residence (Dr. R[obert]. Proust) near the Arc de Triomphe and asked the concierge how I could contact MP.[126]

"It seems everybody wants to contact him[," said the concierge. "]He is a very busy man nowadays, since he has become such a celebrity. I suggest you write him a letter and send it to this address, marked 'fair svivre' [faire suivre, forward] and I will forward it to him." Returning to my hotel I wrote MP a note telling him I was passing through Paris on my return to America and I had only a few days until I would have to catch my boat at Cherbourg, giving him my address.[127] I expected it would take two or three days to get an

123. This hotel was located at 18 rue Papillon, in the ninth arrondissement.

124. As mentioned earlier, the building at 102 boulevard Haussmann was sold to the banker René Varin-Bernier in 1919.

125. In 1914, when Forssgren met Proust, his address at 102 boulevard Haussmann was not secret. In 1919, when Proust was forced to move to new lodgings, only his closest friends, such as Reynaldo Hahn and Lucien Daudet, knew his address. He needed more privacy and also wanted to avoid distracting, meddlesome visitors such as Count Robert de Montesquiou. Proust did have telephone service when Forssgren was there, but, to have fewer interruptions, canceled the service in December 1914, not long after the Swede's departure. *Corr.* 13: 361; Albaret, *Monsieur Proust,* 86.

126. Dr. Robert Proust and his wife Marthe lived at 6 avenue de Messine in the eighth arrondissement, not far from Proust's old address at 102 boulevard Haussmann.

127. Since all the biographical accounts of Proust and Forssgren's

answer. On the second day after I had written I was amazed to find a note he had casually written on the hotel's stationary [*sic*]. Unfortunately, I had been taking in the excitement of Paris and did not get back to the hotel until shortly before 3 AM.[128] I could not believe my ears when the proprietor told me he had waited three or four hours in the chilly damp lobby for my return.[129] He had been gone only a few minutes before I got back. The man told me he was dressed in a heavy fur coat and yet he seemed to be shivering after he had waited some time.[130] The longer he waited, the more he appeared to be growing into a highly emotional, agitated state. He walked around in the lobby continually looking at his watch, acting in such a strange manner, and appeared to be suffering, [so] that the proprietor[131] would look in on him now and again, and finally asked the gentleman if it was anything he could do for him. He declined and told the man he would only wait a few minutes more and then leave if I did not show up. He had

---

missed rendezvous at the Riviera Hotel have been, until now, based on the excerpts published in France in 1975, I will henceforth point out important discrepancies between the original version and the translation. I give in boldface the text omitted by the translation. The translation is quite different here after "through Paris." It reads: "—je devais prendre le bateau pour New York peu après—" (I was to sail to New York shortly). As we see in the original, Forssgren specifies that he was to sail from Cherbourg, which we now know he did around September 27 or 28.

128. The translator rendered Forssgren's "shortly before" as "vers," which means "around."

129. The translator has changed "lobby" to "couloir," "hallway," here and below. It seems obvious that Proust would wait for Forssgren in the lobby and not in the hallway outside his door. It strikes me as improbable that Proust waited three or four hours since he had come by unannounced.

130. The translator changed this to "quelques minutes," a few minutes.

131. The translator here inserted "qu'il fascinait" (who found him fascinating).

impressed the man as being a very important personage. The proprietor also told me he had been in earlier and wanted to know when he thought I might be back.[132] He had told him he thought I had come in about 11 o'clock the previous night.[133] That was probably why he had come back about that time. How my heart sank! How I began to condemn myself! What strange fate! The note read: "Mon cher Ernest, désolé de vous manquer, vous n'etiez pas rentré. Ne venez pas en ce moment ci, mais venez-moi au courant de la date de votre départ. Mille bon souvenirs, Marcel."[134] **He must have been in a great state of confusion, he must have known I did not have his address. It appears he tried to see me as soon as he got my letter, instead of waiting and have me**

132. The translator has changed Forssgren's vague "earlier" to the more precise "dans l'après-midi" (in the afternoon). Given Proust's routine, it is extremely unlikely that he was out and about in the afternoon.

133. The translator made this a direct quotation.

134. Forssgren forgot to completely and correctly copy Proust's note that is reproduced in the French translation and of which the University of Alabama at Birmingham also has a photocopy that Forssgren kept. We do not know what became of the original. The accurate text follows, with the part omitted inadvertently by Forssgren placed in parentheses, followed by the translation of the whole:

Mon cher Ernest, Je suis désolé de vous manquer. Vous n'êtes pas rentré! Ne venez pas en ce moment chez moi, mais tenez-moi au courant de la date de votre départ. (Écrivez-moi hôtel Ritz Place Vendôme, faire suivre.) Mille bons souvenirs, Marcel. [My dear Ernest, sorry to have missed you, you didn't return! Don't come at this time but keep me informed as to the date of your departure. Write me at the hotel Ritz, Place Vendôme, please forward. A thousand good memories, Marcel.]

As part of his strategy for keeping his address at rue Hamelin secret, Proust often used the Ritz Hotel, his favorite hangout, as his mail service. I have translated "mille bons souvenirs" literally since English does not have a corresponding version of this rather standard French complimentary close. The sentiment expressed is "I have many fond memories of the time we spent together."

come to him by sending me a letter, as I took for granted he would, giving me his address. <u>Was he really that anxious and impatient to see me? Was it really possible?</u> Oh, if I had only been in when he called at 11 o'clock! What a world of mystery might have been cleared up. What strange fate! Even had I been back only a few minutes earlier, we would at least have met each other.

Two days later I finally received a letter asking me to come to his apartment in Rue Hamelin.[135] The letter had been delayed a day due to negligence of a hotel employee. It was in the late afternoon. The great moment was at hand. What would our meeting be like? I did not know if Céleste was still with him. The door opened and there she stood,[136] gray as a ghost. She almost appeared in a state of coma, no greeting, and then in a strange sepulchral voice: "C'est vous Ernest, voyez comme je suis restée toujours fidel à monsieur."[137]

"Aren't you going to ask me in?"

"Ah c'est vrai, entrez donc." [Ah, that's true, do come in.][138]

She ushered me into the salon next to the foyer and asked me to sit down. She went on telling me how successful MP had been. His health had improved after the war and he had even put on weight.[139]

135. The whereabouts of this letter is unknown. Proust's last apartment, in which he lived from October 1919 until his death, was at 44 rue Hamelin, in the sixteenth arrondissement.

136. The translator added the word *raide* [stiff] to the description of Céleste.

137. C'est vous, Ernest? Voyez comme je suis restée toujours fidèle à monsieur. [It's you, Ernest? See how I have always remained faithful to monsieur.] The translator has rendered "always faithful," as "Je suis toujours là" [I'm still here].

138. Céleste does not mention this visit in her memoirs.

139. The translator has changed the text here: "Sa santé avait été dure-

"How is he now?" I asked. **"I have written him and he has asked me to come and see him, and here I am."**

Her mind seemed then to become in great turmoil. There was a strange fear in her eyes. Her speech became rather incoherent. "Oh, Ernest, an unbelievable thing has happened. A few nights ago he went out against his doctor's strict standing orders, not to ever expose himself to the damp Paris night air, on some 'mysterious visit.' He was gone several hours and did not get back until 3 AM. I was worried about him and heard him when he came in. What on earth could have induced him to take such a risk, and stay away so long? C'est incroyable. [It's unbelievable.] The doctors are with him now; he is in one of his worst crises. He has had to be given sedatives."[140]

Suddenly, the door to his chamber opened and the doctors came out **talking and gesticulating excitedly.** I could hear fragments of their conversation: "mais je l'ais pourtant défendus . . . sous paine da mort . . . pourquoi . . . jen'on sais rien . . . **il ne explique pas . . . C'est incroyable . . .** ".[141]

---

ment mise à l'épreuve par la guerre, et il ne s'en était jamais vraiment remis." [The war was very hard on his health and he never really got over it.]

140. Céleste left two detailed accounts of Proust's final days, one in a filmed interview (1962) and one in her memoirs. They are consistent. (For excerpts from the film interview with Céleste, see the documentary film made for American television, *Marcel Proust: A Writer's Life*.) This dialogue with Céleste seems to be pure invention since we now know that Forssgren left France before the onset of Proust's final illness. Ellis Island records show that he boarded the *Majestic* in Cherbourg and arrived in New York harbor on October 2, 1922. The immigration manifest is dated October 3, 1922. The *Majestic* normally made the transatlantic run in five or six days, which would place his departure from Cherbourg on September 26 or 27.

141. "mais je l'avais pourtant défendu . . . sous peine de mort . . . pourquoi . . . je n'en sais rien . . . il n'explique pas . . . C'est incroyable . . ." [but moreover I forbade him . . . under pain of death . . . why . . . I know nothing about it . . . he doesn't explain. . . . It's unbelievable . . .]

Just then the doorbell rang and Céleste went to answer. It was Docteur Robert Proust, his brother.[142]

"How is he now, can I see him?" [Dr. Proust asked one of the doctors.]

"No one can see him, he is in a bad way, I am afraid, very much afraid it might be the beginning of the end."[143]

"What about this visit he made that time of night? What could have been so important, or rather who could have meant so much to him that he would risk his already precarious health that way?" his brother wanted to know.

The feeling that came over me was something I had never experienced before. I felt like a criminal, **like a potential murderer.** Here I was sitting, obviously unobserved, **fortunately,** with all the answers to all the questions. I wanted to leave immediately. I was in such a state of emotion I could not face Céleste without betraying myself. **She was being given some instructions by** the doctors **and the two of them** and Dr. Proust departed. As Céleste returned [from

142. If there were already "doctors" present when Dr. Robert Proust arrived, that would make at least three doctors in the apartment. The only time Proust was ill enough to require the attendance of several doctors was on the day he died: November 18, 1922, nearly two months after Forssgren sailed back to the United States.

143. No medical colleague would have told Dr. Proust, a distinguished physician and scientist, that he could not see his brother, especially if Proust was in agony. At most, he would have conveyed Proust's wishes that he not be disturbed. As one would expect, during Proust's final hours, it was Robert Proust who took over the sickroom and issued the orders. During the days preceding his death, Proust stubbornly refused to yield to the entreaties of his closest, lifelong friend, the composer Reynaldo Hahn, who urged him, in a moving letter, to cooperate with his brother and enter a health clinic where he could receive proper treatment. For a description of Proust's final days, see William C. Carter, *Marcel Proust: A Life* (New Haven: Yale University Press, 2000), 799–810.

seeing them out] I bade her a hasty au revoir and told her how sorry I was about MP's condition and not being able to see him. I would call back later to inquire about MP.[144] **I was hoping she had not guessed my secret, or if she managed to add two and two, and the coincidence of my visit just then, and should ask herself if it could have any connection with the fatal night visit, "la visite mystérieuse" [the** mysterious visit]—**if so, I was hoping she would keep her secret as well as I would keep mine.**

The following days were filled with anxiety. My heart never felt heavier. Just think if he should die? The doctor had said, "I am afraid it is the beginning of the end." **And what will that make of me?**

Wishfully thinking and hoping against hope that the state of affairs were [*sic*] not as serious as they seemed, I wrote MP a note stating I had called **on him as he had invited me [to], and found he was not able to see me then, and if his condition was induced by the dangerous night visit to my hotel,** I asked him to try to understand my deep feeling of culpability, my deep sympathy, and would he forgive me.[145] I blamed a cruel fate that had prevented us from meeting again

144. The translator rendered "I would call back" as "Je téléphonerais," but as we have seen, Proust had not had a telephone since late 1914. Once the telephone service was stopped, Céleste had to go to a nearby café to make his calls for him. From here to the end of the paragraph, the translator has altered the text and omitted the words that provided the title that Forssgren gave his memoir: "Je partis en souhaitant de tout mon cœur, mais sans trop y croire, qu'elle ne devine pas mon douloureux secret: j'espérais qu'elle garderait au moins le silence." [I left, wishing with all my heart, but without really believing it, that she would not guess my sorrowful secret: I hoped that she would at least keep silent.]

145. Part of this is omitted, part altered in the translation: "la visite m'avait été interdite, comme à tout un chacun" [I had not been allowed to see him, like everyone else].

after all these **anxious** years.[146] I congratulated him on his great success confirming my faith in him as a great future author, when I first read his initial work "Du côté de chez Swann" [*Swann's Way*] of which he so kindly presented me with a copy, inscribed and autographed for me, and which I treasure as one of my most precious possessions.[147] I expressed hopes that he would soon be well, and if I would not be able to see him this time, I expected to be back in Paris not later than next spring, and I would be looking forward with great pleasure and anticipation [to] our meeting then. My ship would be leaving in a few days and in the meanwhile I would inquire about his health.[148] "The memory of your warm and generous heart, your kindness and sincerity, shall always be with me through life. Au revoir until we meet next spring." I mentioned I had not spoken of his visit to anyone.

I would call at Dr. Proust's and inquire of the concierge how MP was doing.[149] It seemed his condition was worsening. He was never able to see anybody. It was the day I was to leave **for New York.**[150] I decided to make a last call on Céleste

146. "I blamed" is translated as "Je m'enrageais" [I was enraged].

147. Proust gave Forssgren the signed copy in 1914. See Forssgren's "Summary," where Forssgren reveals that he had not been able to read *Du côté de chez Swann*. By 1922 the following sections of the novel had been published: *À l'ombre des jeunes filles en fleurs*, which won the Goncourt Prize in 1919, *Le Côté de Guermantes* (1920), and *Sodome et Gomorrhe* (1921). The remaining volumes were to be published posthumously: *La Prisonnière*, *La Fugitive* (also known *as Albertine disparue*), and *Le Temps retrouvé*. Forssgren gives the inscription Proust wrote in his copy of *Du côté de chez Swann* at the end of the memoirs.

148. The translation of the departure is less precise: "n'allait pas tarder à lever l'ancre" [would be weighing anchor soon].

149. Again "would call" is translated as "telephone," whereas it is clear that Forssgren intends to call in person.

150. The translator removed the important indication of Forssgren's port of entry: New York.

and tell her good-bye, also telling her I would be back in the spring and hoped to see her and MP then. "I am afraid," she said, "that MP may not live till then. He is sinking every day. I told him of your visit, when he had recovered somewhat, and he wrote you a last letter under great stress and utmost effort. I hope you received it."

We bade each other good-bye, but it did not seem as our hearts were in it. There was a discordant note somewhere. **Could it be that jealousy had foiled me here too? What is more painful than doubt? What is more unjust than doubt and jealousy?** But it was I that was at fault, **my doubt, my unfair suspicion.** Céleste was incapable of perfidy. As I got back to my hotel there was the letter from MP.[151] I also received a bon voyage telegram from MP.[152]

The following afternoon I boarded the ship that was to take me back to the great land of promise, of opportunity. I was returning with a heavy heart. What was my fate to be? "Making

151. The letter is lost. A fragment of it was published in the *Études proustiennes,* based on a fragmentary photocopy that the editors saw; they say the date was clearly legible as September 19. (For the contents of the surviving portion of this letter, see Forssgren's "Summary.") Forssgren speaks of a "bon voyage" telegram in the singular. The telegram now in the University of Alabama at Birmingham collection bears the clear date of September 1, which does not fit well with the chronology of a "bon voyage" message since Forssgren was not to depart for several weeks. Perhaps Proust was uncertain of that date and did not feel well enough to anticipate being able to see Forssgren before his departure. The most important revelation contained in this telegram is that Proust gave his address as 44 rue Hamelin, which means that it was written after the note left at the Riviera Hotel, the occasion of "the mysterious visit," in which note Proust tells Forssgren to write to him in care of the Ritz Hotel. Forssgren raises the issue of the date of the "mysterious visit" in his "Summary."

152. Here the French excerpts end and the translator summarizes in a single sentence Forssgren's conclusion, that after he returned to New York, his sister in Stockholm sent news of Proust's death.

money," a filthy, detestable phrase, or becoming a useful, creative citizen and develope [*sic*] the talents I knew I possessed? If only MP would recover. He must recover. I was born to be a professor of languages, beautiful languages, THE LATIN LANGUAGES, with any other language I couldn't be bothered.

The sea voyage promised to be a delightful one for the peaceful mind. For the mind in turmoil, in doubt and anxiety, it was a question of jumping over-board or having a little more patience, patience to wait for the final outcome. [I thought,] "Whatever happens, Ernest, you are still young, you have your health, even though your ear buzzes, you have your life ahead of you." I could have had a very enjoyable sea journey but I refused it. I kept to myself. I did not want to mix with anyone. I became a loner. I wanted, and managed, to get a table to myself. I came to be regarded as a strange character for such a young man, a killjoy. I heard remarks. I was sought, but I shunned. My apprehension of tragedy was my only companion. My days passed in gloom in spite of gaiety surrounding me. The ship landed and after clearing the customs I took a taxi to the YMCA, my usual habitat in New York. I had given this as my permanent address in New York to my relatives in Sweden.

I had been back only a short time when I received a letter from my sister V. with the tragic news, a clipping from a Stockholm newspaper, announcing the death of Marcel Proust, the famous French writer, "LE DERNIER CRI."[153]

The last gasp as far as I was concerned. Something within me died then and there. My ambition, my career, gone. Half of me died. Had my soul died? Was my physical being only to carry me on through life? Should I just go on "making

153. Assuming that Forssgren's sister wrote him immediately after Proust's death and that the letter took a minimum of three weeks to reach him in New York, he received the news at the earliest two months after his return to the United States.

money," or should I go back to Paris and carry on by myself and try to do what I originally set out to do? To be a human with a soul or "make money?" With this dismal, discordant note I shall end this Narrative.

I am, most sorrowfully, forced to the tragic conclusion that had it not been for the "MYSTERIOUS VISIT," Marcel Proust might have lived on many more productive years. I have in my possession the note he left at my hotel, the last letter he wrote me, probably the last letter he ever wrote, the telegram he sent me the day I left Paris, a copy of his first edition of "DU COTE DE CHEZ SWANN," inscribed: "À Ernst Forssgren, en témoignage de mon parfait [ma parfaite] estime, et de mon cordial souvenir, Marcel Proust"; also his photograph similarly inscribed.[154] ALL TRAGIC REMINDERS OF WHAT MIGHT HAVE BEEN. I will ask the reader to please bear in mind that the ideas, thoughts, opinions, impressions, expressions, actions and reactions, as conveyed in this account, are those of a young man of the time, the epoch that this narrative covers which are the years 1913 to 1922.[155]

It is regrettable that I did not keep a diary during the time I was with Monsieur Proust. I am writing this entire account from memory, in retrospect; therefore it is possible it may contain some unintentional inaccuracies and discrepancies.[156]

154. "To Ernst Forssgren, as proof of my perfect esteem and fond memory." The date of the September 1 telegram allows us to establish with more precision the chronology of events and determine that the "mysterious visit" is not the occasion when Proust caught his final illness. We have more than fifty letters that Proust wrote after the last one to Forssgren on September 19. For a discussion of this and the contents of the telegram, see Forssgren's "Summary."

155. Forssgren inadvertently repeated "actions and" on the top of the next sheet of paper.

156. Since Forssgren had no contact with anyone who knew Proust who

Epilogue

This story constitutes a small part from the life of a sad, embittered old man who wasted his life, who lives ONLY by virtue of a still vigorous sense of HUMOR. E.A.F.

HIS ONLY ASSET

This narrative I dedicate to the memory of Marcel Proust, the truest friend I ever knew. The man who accepted, recognized, no other aristocracy, nobility, but that of the soul.[157]

---

could have given him details about the writer's final illness and death, he may have come to believe that what he wrote was the truth. Céleste and others who knew Proust well were still alive in 1965, when Forssgren wrote this memoir. Had his relationship with Céleste been as friendly as he claimed, he could certainly have obtained the details from her. Or he could easily have contacted them or the Proust Society (Société des Amis de Marcel Proust) founded in 1950.

157. Forssgren may not have read Proust, but this remark is certainly true. This "nobility of the soul" is represented in his novel chiefly by the character of the grandmother, a modest, altruistic woman who is described at one point as bearing what Proust considered to be one of the most important virtues, that of "natural distinction."

Afterword

⬦ ⬦ ⬦

SOMETIME after his return to the United States, Ernest Forssgren headed west to California. The 1930 U.S. Census Records show him living in Los Angeles, where his good looks had landed him a movie contract with Jack Warner. His movie career, like his other ambitions, faltered; Forssgren was never called before the cameras. He later owned land in Los Angeles and operated a motel there, but his real estate ventures did not bring him success either. In the spring of 1966, apparently disgusted with life in the United States, he decided to return to *la belle France* and settled in Provence. He was no happier there than he had been in the States. In less than a year he returned to California, where he was to die several years later at the age of seventy-six.

—W.C.C.

Forssgren's "Summary" of Painter

❖   ❖   ❖

What follows is the text of Ernest Forssgren's summary of his reaction to George D. Painter's two-volume biography of Proust. The first volume was *Proust: The Early Years* (Boston: Little, Brown, 1959), the second *Proust: The Later Years* (Boston: Little, Brown, 1965). It is apparent from the date of Forssgren's memoirs, 1965, and from the notes written in his copy of volume 2 of Painter, that it was this publication that enraged him and inspired him to write his memoirs. He typed his summary of Painter, single-spaced, on both sides of a piece of $8\frac{1}{2} \times 11$ onionskin paper, folded it in half twice, and left it in his copy of *Proust: The Later Years*. He corrected some of the misspelled words by hand, indicating that he read it over again. This statement, like the memoirs, was written before Céleste Albaret's memoirs were published. The few details Forssgren gives about the departure for Cabourg with Proust and Céleste and the stay there seem more reflective than the account given in his memoirs. My additions are in brackets; my comments follow the text.

139

S
UMMARY of my impression and opinion of the book "Biography" of the life of Marcel Proust, "The Later Years," by George D. Painter. E.A.F.

After a sporadic, skippingly fragmentary perusal of the above mentioned alleged "biography," this incomprehensible, nonsensical drivel, perpetrated by this certain Painter I would suggest his immediate return to house painting.

As I would judge by this persons [*sic*] picture he must have been born about the time of the death of Marcel Proust.[1] Where does he get his data? Certainly not first hand nor second hand. He must have gotten the material from a dozen or more sources. It strikes me that most of it consists of M.P.'s own "autobiography," changed, rehashed and rephrased so as to pass for an authentic biography by a competent and expert biographer. How many would know the difference? I would say it is mostly a substitution of the first person with a third person, if the reader gets what I mean.

What is it but a pedantic description, recital of the doings of a parasitic coterie of idle rich and sundry aristocracy, royalty and what have you, their dilletantism, their wild pursuit of pleasure, and what pleasures? according to the said "biography". Mostly sex in all its devious forms, and perhaps even normal, and it goes without saying, accompanied with alcohol and every sort of narcotica. The story is so rambling and disconnected that it is impossible to make sense of what is read. I take it that it is absolutely necessary to have read all of M.P.'s works to understand it. I make no critisism of M.P. as I have never read his works. It is true that I started to read "Du côté de chez Swann," but my french vocubulary was too limmited at the time, and that subject too deep for the under-

1. George Duncan Painter was born in 1914 and died in 2005.

standing of a young man of twenty years, but I did get the impression that M.P. was a gifted writer.

I want to point out here that it was only a few short months that I became acquainted with M.P. and then only in the capacity of his valet de chambre. When I answered his ad as I describe in my story, I had never heard of M.P. and did not know any more of him than he about me.[2] I did not stay in his apartment in Paris until we came back from Cabourg. I went direct from Prince Orloff to his apartment and then to the train the same day. It was a great emergency for M.P. and myself. We had to leave Paris as fast as possible, but it was a lucky break for me.

This alleged homosexuality on the part of M.P. which G.D.P. alludes to I certainly had no knowledge of, and I find it hard to believe. He definitely made no overtures to me in that direction, and I saw no signs of any such activity on his part. We had a suite of three rooms adjoining all connecting with each other, doors between each room. M.P.'s room first, nearest the elevator, then Madame Céleste's room next to his, and then mine. If he had visitors after I left him, usually 8 or 9 o'clock, I knew nothing about it. He would always have M.C. [Madame Céleste] call me when he wanted me, and he would always tell me when he wanted me to leave. In no way would I impose on his time. Since I worked four hours about, in the hospital, I would only spend three or four hours with him. He was very anxious for me to prepare myself to become his secretary as soon as possible. He would have me read his M.S. [manuscript] so as to acquaint myself with his hand writing, and it was planned he would buy a typrwriter [sic] as

2. This sentence indicates that Forssgren wrote the "Summary" after the memoirs.

soon as we got back to Paris, and I would start writing [typing] his manuscripts.[3] There was one little insident that had set my mind awandering, sort of vaguely. Some friends, he had quite a number of them in Cabourg[,] had brought him a lot of books. He handed me, one afternoon, a book by Oscar Wilde The "De Profundis" and wanted to know what I thought of it, after reading. I had never heard of O.W. much less read any of his works. I could see right away it was much too profundis for me, at least I could not get interested, and returned it to M.P. I had learned that he had written the book in prison, so I asked M.P. Why he had been imprisoned and he explained evrything to me. Well, that's where my religious uppbringing asserted itself and I told M.P., in my naivety, in no uncertain terms what I thought. Then a sudden idea occurred to me, perhaps, could it be, was it an attempt to find out where I stood, as regards that certain delicate subject, if so it was an extremely subtle hint. And if so . . . I didnot [*sic*] want to offend him, I modified my rash verbal outburst by saying "chaque un a son gout" [Chacun à son goût], each one to his own taste.

In that book by G.D.P. there is a rather curious coincident. The much mentioned Albert Le Cuziat: pages 262–71, 276, 282, 302, 306, 354, was first footman at prince Orloff, (in the book referred to as coutn [*sic*] Orloff, perhaps because M.P. did not know prince Orloff personally, the only connection being Le Cuziat).[4] I certainly had no idea he was leading

---

3. Proust had purchased a typewriter for Agostinelli to type the manuscript of *Swann's Way* soon after his former chauffeur became his secretary in late May 1913. Proust sold the typewriter to Larue's restaurant after Agostinelli's abrupt departure in early December 1913. For the details of the Proust-Agostinelli relationship, see William C. Carter, *Proust in Love* (New Haven: Yale University Press, 2006).

4. Forssgren did not close the parentheses.

a double life. He was very friendly and seemed a regular guy. He was the one who gave me the nick name "Le Parisien[.]" About one third of the people, the aristocracy and royalty mentioned in the book[,] were friends of Prince Orloff. Especially the Duchesse d'Uzès, a very frequent visitor at prince Orloff's. Some of the names are among the most "illustrous" in France. Enough of that, it is all <u>so unimportant</u>. I could not possibly wade through all that. I find it utterly boring. I'd rather read about Mrs. Rileys cow.[5]

Some day, maybe I will read M.P.'s works. That title "Sodom & Gomorra" is rather frightening.[6] I picture it as description of the modern universal "Sodom & Gomorra", such as the whole world is today, patterned after the "local" ancient "Sodom & Gomorra", a small mild version of [the] universal one of today. . . .[7] I am sorry but it won't be long now. What is soon to be <u>will be</u>. The law of cause and effect is infallible.

Spending billions and billions sending men in capsules around the earth, soon the moon, mars, the sun etc. IS THERE ANYTHING TO EQUAL MAN'S FOLLY? A relatively small fraction of the cost of carrying out man's unbelievable, incredible folly, UNSPEAKABLE FOLLY, could put the world, the whole world in order so that man could live in peace and abundance. This mystic power we call "satan" has taken over, completely. Let man spend himself.

5. Forssgren presumably means Mrs. O'Leary's cow that, according to legend, started the Great Chicago Fire in 1871.

6. This is the fourth section of *In Search of Lost Time* and contains many pages involving homosexuality, a subject considered taboo at the time of its publication in two volumes in 1921 and 1922.

7. The ellipsis is Forssgren's. Is he thinking particularly of the San Francisco of the 1960s, his home when he wrote the memoirs? That city was and remains a mecca for homosexuals.

BUT THE GREAT MYSTIC POWER WE CALL GOD WILL FINALLY
PREVAIL.

Science can create machinery that can send men to the
planets, but [is] unable to create the formula for peace and
brotherly love. There is abundance for all the people on
earth, if man would only work for construction instead of
desrtuction [sic]. AMEN.

This, what I have stated here is my personal opinion, My
impression.

MISANTHROPOLOS

In the memoirs, as we have seen, Forssgren uses his real name,
although at the end he speaks of being "a sad, embittered old
man." His "Summary" of Painter is signed Misanthropolos, the
pseudonym he sometimes used on the return address of letters
to friends as an indication of the profound misanthrope that he
had become.

While professing shock at Painter's mention of "devious"
sexuality, Forssgren denies knowledge of such activity on
Proust's part or of the "double life" that Albert Le Cuziat was
leading. Since he admits not having read Proust, he is unable to
speak about the many pages in the novel devoted to homosexuality. Yet those who knew Forssgren well in later life describe
him as homosexual, confirming what those who have studied
Proust and his milieu had long assumed. For example, Christian Pechenard, in his book on Proust at Cabourg, writes,
rather unkindly, in a passage describing the advantage of having
a servant from a neutral nation during time of war: "Ernest
Forssgren était idiot mais homosexuel et suédois."[8] The remark
about his "stupidity" is presumably based on Céleste's negative
remarks regarding the valet.

What strikes one in comparing the memoirs with the "Summary" is that in the lengthy recollections of the first, there is no
hint of homosexuality at all and that Forssgren eagerly depicts

8. "Ernest Forssgren was stupid but homosexual and Swedish." *Proust
à Cabourg* (Paris: Quai Voltaire, 1992), 165.

himself as someone Proust was extraordinarily fond of and with whom he intended to spend much time in private while grooming the young Swede to become his secretary. The only remark that might be taken as a reference to a possible homosexual link between Forssgren and Proust is the brother's admission that he did not forward Proust's letter because he did not want Ernest to associate with the French writer. Presumably, as we have said, this was his brother Alfred, who also worked as a valet for Prince Orloff. If that is what the brother had in mind—and it's difficult to imagine what else it might be—Forssgren clearly decided to avoid the scandalous topic at that point in the memoirs. Earlier in the memoirs he describes Proust's embraces, usually interrupted by Céleste, who comes barging in just in time. In her memoirs, Céleste writes that she was instructed never to knock on Proust's door and not to come to his room unless summoned. She tells of her anxiety once, at boulevard Haussmann, when she waited for nearly two days for Proust to ring the bell that called her to his room. Convinced that he lay dead beyond the door of the cork-lined chamber, she still did not dare to violate the rule and waited until at long last the bell sounded. (This scene is vividly re-created in Percy Adlon's feature film *Céleste*.)[9]

The routine at the Grand-Hôtel in Cabourg, as described in Forssgren's "Summary," is in keeping with what we know from other sources about Proust's habits and therefore appears more accurate: that Forssgren knew nothing about any visitors after 8 or 9 in the evening, that Céleste summoned him on Proust's behalf, and that Proust always dismissed him when he had no further need of him.

It seems likely that Forssgren raises the issue of homosexuality in the "Summary" because he realized that, given Painter's volume 2, he could not avoid doing so—having spoken so often to friends about his connection with the famous writer—even though Painter was unaware of Forssgren's existence or even

9. See "Deux jours d'angoisse" [Two days of anxiety], a short chapter in Céleste Albaret, *Monsieur Proust,* as told to Georges Belmont (Paris: Éditions Robert Laffont, 1973), 333–38.

that a third individual had accompanied Proust and Céleste to Cabourg. Ernest broaches the topic to express his surprise and disapproval, and to deny any knowledge that Proust was homosexual. Although there is no mention of Oscar Wilde's *De Profundis* in Proust's known letters and writings, I am inclined to believe what Forssgren says about the use of this book to test his reaction, primarily because of Forssgren's admitted lack of interest in reading works other than such popular novels as *The Count of Monte Cristo*. In short, it is difficult to imagine his being aware of Wilde's book otherwise. There are references and allusions to Wilde in Proust's letters and writings, but none to that specific work.[10]

Wilde wrote *De Profundis* in 1897, while serving his prison term in Reading Gaol. The book gives no indication that he is incarcerated for having committed acts of sodomy. Wilde speaks poignantly of having "disgraced . . . eternally" the family name after having been "to many the arbiter of style in art; the supreme arbiter to some." At one point Wilde describes (very obliquely, and hence in a way that Forssgren could not have understood, even if he read that far) evenings spent at a London hotel with young male prostitutes: "People thought it dreadful of me to have entertained at dinner the evil things of life, and to have found pleasure in their company. But then, from the point of view through which I, as an artist in life, approach them they were delightfully suggestive and stimulating. It was like feasting with panthers."[11]

Although Forssgren admits in the "Summary" that he found Proust too difficult to read, he does know, probably from Painter, the title *Sodom and Gomorrah*, which he finds "frightening." In the opening pages of that part of the novel, Proust alludes to Wilde without naming him. This reference occurs at the beginning of what is said to be the longest sentence in liter-

---

10. For an account of the brief encounter between Oscar Wilde (1854–1900) and the connection between Wilde and Proust's treatment of homosexuality in *In Search of Lost Time*, see Carter, *Proust in Love*.

11. See Oscar Wilde, *De Profundis* (London: Methuen, 1905), 33, 39, 144–45.

ature. The Narrator is speaking about the plight of homosexuals who must live in a society that condemns them: "Their hon-
our precarious, their liberty provisional, lasting only until the
discovery of their crime; their position unstable, like that of the
poet one day fêted in every drawing-room and applauded in
every theatre in London, and the next driven from every lodg-
ing, unable to find a pillow upon which to lay his head, turning
the mill like Samson and saying like him: 'The two sexes shall
die, each in a place apart.'"[12]

Painter tells his readers that "Wilde's fall" is "mentioned" in
Sodom and Gomorrah and gives the page number.[13] Forssgren
made no marginal marks in his copy of Painter on the several
pages where the Irish writer is named. Forssgren may simply
have skipped those pages or may have forgotten about them by
the time he wrote his "Summary." We have no way to judge the
sincerity of Forssgren's surprise at Painter's revelation of Albert
Le Cuziat's role as the proprietor of male brothels.

12. *Sodom and Gomorrah* 4: 21. In Charles K. Scott Moncrieff's English
translation the sentence contains 958 words. The quotation, "Les deux
sexes mourront chacun de son côté," is from Alfred de Vigny's poem "La
Colère de Samson" [The wrath of Samson]. Vigny's poem also provided the
epigraph for *Sodom and Gomorrah:* "La femme aura Gomorrhe et l'homme
aura Sodome" [The women shall have Gomorrah and the men shall have
Sodom]. *Sodom and Gomorrah* 4: 1.

13. Painter, *Proust*, 2: 107 and n. 2.

Forssgren's Marginalia

❖　❖　❖

Forssgren wrote these comments in his copy of *Proust: The Later Years*, volume 2 of Painter's biography of Marcel Proust (Boston: Little, Brown, first American edition, 1965). All page references below are to this volume. We do not know whether Forssgren owned a copy of volume 1, *Proust: The Early Years*. The book jacket is missing. Forssgren made his notations in pencil; those on the inside covers were partially erased afterward, making some words illegible.

Inside Front Cover

This book is, at least 50 per cent fraud, an alleged "biography." This alleged [illegible] least [illegible] 75 per cent fraud. Shows what people get away with nowadays.

Inside Back Cover

As I have said many times, anyone who has anything good to say about the english whatsoever, is a Goddamn liar. I take [?] the british [illegible] the english [illegible] What I think [?][illegible] of the english words fail me.

The english foisted too [*sic*] world wars on us and is busy with a third. England <u>cannot</u> exist without wars. There will always be english provided that we <u>always have wars</u>.

Marginalia

Dates given after chapter titles are Painter's.

CHAPTER 10, AGOSTINELLI VANISHES
(September 1913–July 1914)

Page 199. Next to the publication date of *Du côté de chez Swann,* Forssgren writes: "The edition of which M.P. inscribed and autographed a copy for me."

CHAPTER 11, THE DEATH OF SAINT-LOUP
(August 1914–January 1916)

Page 219. Regarding the number of the room Proust occupied at Cabourg, which Painter gives as "No. 147," Forssgren writes: "What God damn lies!! He had a suite of rooms, his, Céleste's and my room, in a row."[1] Forssgren seems not to take

---

1. Painter's source for the room number is not clear. His bibliography does not list any of the interviews given by Céleste Albaret prior to his biography. In her memoirs (1973), she gives the room number as 137, although she admits she is not certain. This number is probably not correct, since Proust always took rooms on the top floor. Two paragraphs below the one in which she tries to recall the room number, Céleste writes, "We went directly up to the top floor, where three rooms were reserved, all overlooking the sea. Above, there was another terrace, but because of M. Proust, no one was allowed to use it throughout his stay." Céleste Albaret, *Monsieur Proust,* as told to Georges Belmont, trans. Barbara Bray (New York: New York Review of Books, 2003), 30, 31. In the year following the trip to Cabourg, Proust said

into account that the room number, whatever it was, does not contradict his and Céleste's description of the suite of rooms. He makes another notation, confirming the presence of wounded soldiers: "Hospital was first two floors of Grand Hotel." This is another indication that the rooms used by Proust were on the upper floors, the third or the fourth, and hence numbered in the 300s or 400s.

Page 220. Where Painter writes, "About 12 October, all his [Proust's] money spent on gifts for the soldiers, he returned to Paris," Forssgren comments, "Although there was no checking account those days he could raise any amount of money at any time any where." Forssgren is simply wrong here; Proust and Céleste both relate the suspension of normal banking business and the impossibility of obtaining ready cash. Regarding the date of October 12, 1914, Forssgren observes: "It was later than October 12.—we left [sentence not finished] Not true. I was there." Forssgren continues his thoughts about the money problem on the bottom on p. 221. "To have made all those gifts he would have had to send me to buy them." This is an interesting point, because one cannot imagine Proust doing such errands by himself. Perhaps he used one of the many staff available at the Grand-Hôtel. Forssgren writes: "The only gifts the soldiers got were the

---

in a letter to a friend that he preferred to be on the fourth level of the Grand-Hôtel at Cabourg, high above the sea, where he thought it was much dryer even than on the third floor. In his travels, he often took the top floor, not only because he believed the elevation gave him extra protection from dust and pollen in the air but also because there could be no one walking or making other noises on the floor above. See *Corr.* 21: 662. The hotel records for the years of Proust's vacations there, 1907–14, have not survived. In recent years the hotel re-created room 414 as "Proust's room." Based on what we know about Proust's preferences, this seems a much better guess than 137 or 147.

ones I gave." We see that Céleste, Forssgren, and Proust all disagree here. According to Céleste, there were no soldiers and therefore no gifts. Proust claims that he paid for and presented the gifts. Forssgren maintains that he presented them. Proust seems to hold the trump card here. He witnessed a scene at Cabourg that he described in a letter several months after the stay at the Grand-Hôtel, a scene that he later used, in an entirely different setting, in *Within a Budding Grove*. Here again is the original incident, as described by Proust to Reynaldo Hahn's sister, Madame de Madrazo:

At Cabourg—I don't know whether I told the story to Reynaldo—one day when I brought some draught sets to the black soldiers (Senegalese and Moroccans) who are fond of that game, a very stupid lady (there seem to be a particularly large number of them at Cabourg) came to stare at them as though they were quaint animals and said to one of them: "Good morning nigger" which offended him horribly. "Me nigger," he retorted, "you old cow." When I brought the wounded a few dozen packs of playing-cards they complained that they weren't poker sets (with jokers if that's the right word). I returned with the packs in question, and then they complained that they couldn't play bridge.[2]

Proust often used his letters, as he did his late-night conversations with Céleste, as rehearsals for what he would write in the novel. Christian Pechenard, in his book on Proust at Cabourg, sides with Céleste and maintains that the first wounded arrived at the hotel in the spring of 1915, long after Proust's departure. His source for this information is not, however, any hard evidence but the testimony of a retired schoolteacher, Jean Bayle, citing his childhood recollections. Bayle's father had been

2. SL 3: 297. For the transposition of this scene in the novel, see *Within a Budding Grove* 2: 148–49.

a stagehand at the casino of the Grand-Hôtel when the war began.[3]

Page 223. Forssgren underlined part of a sentence by Painter regarding Proust's health after the Cabourg trip: "he was by now permanently unfit, both in body and in mind, for any way of life other <u>than insomnia, asthma, fumigation, and confinement to bed for six and a half days in every week.</u>" Forssgren writes in the margin: "How could he have gone to the 'hospital' every day with gifts to the soldiers?" This, too, is an excellent point and an indication that Forssgren is reading carefully. Here it is Painter who is wrong about Proust's health. Could Painter's portrait of a sedentary Proust have influenced Forssgren's similar depiction in his memoirs? Proust's letters and Céleste's memoirs show that in 1914 the novelist led a fairly active life and was not confined to bed for such long periods.

CHAPTER 13, THE PIT OF SODOM
(March 1917–November 1918)

Page 263. Forssgren corrects Painter's "Count" Orloff to "Prince" Orloff.

CHAPTER 17, THE TWO WAYS MEET
(September–November 1922)

Page 353. Near the bottom of the page, at Painter's sentence "Towards the middle of September he ventured several times to the Ritz for his four a.m. dinner," Forssgren notes: "It was the 15th of September he made 'The Mysterious Visit.'[4] Ac-

3. See Christian Pechenard, *Proust à Cabourg* (Paris: Quai Voltaire, 1992), 168.

4. The editors of excerpts published in *Études proustiennes* say that Painter gives October 19 as the date of the "mysterious visit" and that his

cording to Céleste he had been feeling relatively fine until then." Forssgren is apparently taking the date of September 15 from Painter, and forgetting the evidence, in his own possession, regarding the date of Proust's "mysterious visit" to the Riviera Hotel. This evidence is found in the recently discovered telegram that Proust sent Forssgren. It is postmarked (telegrams were sent from the post office) September 1, 1922, rue Bleue 14e (the postal station closest to the Riviera Hôtel), and is addressed to Ernest Forssgren, Riviera Hôtel, 18 rue Papillon. It reads "Mon cher Ernest, Il m'est impossible de vous voir étant donné le court délai que vous me fixez donc mes adieux. Mes amitiés, Marcel

---

source was presumably an interview given by Céleste on November 20, 1952. However, there are two problems here. First, Painter does indeed mention that date but does not describe it as a mysterious visit. In fact, he gives no details about it at all. Here is what Painter writes: "Late on the afternoon of the 19th [of October] Proust disobeyed his doctor and his fever, dressed and went out for the last time. His strength failed, and he returned almost immediately, cold to the marrow, shuddering, racked with fits of sinister sneezing" (356). Forssgren enclosed this paragraph in pencil marks but gave no comment, surely in part because there are no details in Painter on which to comment. Proust's actions here are the imaginings of Painter. The second problem with the note in *Études proustiennes* is that the assumed source, Céleste's 1952 interview, does not contain a word or any hint about the "mysterious visit." This is indeed the source given by Painter for the October 19 sortie, but there is nothing in her interview about October 19 or anything to do with a mysterious visit. If the editors, in establishing their chronology for the visit, had checked Painter's source, they would have discovered it to be nonexistent. There are no precise dates—only months—mentioned in Céleste's interview describing Proust's last illness. She says, "En septembre, Marcel ne se rase plus" [In September, Marcel stopped shaving]. Here we can suspect the interviewer, who also commits a number of other errors. Céleste never called Proust "Marcel." The next month she mentions is November: "On est en novembre" [Now we are in November]. For the interview in question, see "Trente ans après. Céleste, servante au grand coeur, nous raconte les derniers jours de Proust" [Thirty years later. Céleste, the big-hearted servant, tells us about Proust's last days], *Nouvelles littéraires,* November 20 1952, 1–2.

(PS) Si vous aviez à m'écrire ou à me téléphoner adressez votre lettre à mon nom 44, rue Hamelin."[5]

The date of the telegram means that the "mysterious visit" by Proust to the Riviera Hotel must have taken place earlier because, in the note left at the hotel, Proust did not give Forssgren his address on rue Hamelin but instructed him to send his letters to the Ritz Hotel for forwarding. The use of the Ritz as a mail drop would be pointless if Forssgren already had his address. Therefore, Proust's attempt to see Forssgren at the Riviera Hotel must have taken place shortly before September 1. The telegram is apparently the reply to a letter that Forssgren sent to Proust in care of the Ritz Hotel, saying that he would be departing soon and wished to see him.

The missing letter sent to Forssgren on September 19, of which only a fragmentary photocopy survives, begins with Proust describing his temporary residence in 1919 at 8 bis rue Laurent-Pichat. With workmen due to begin renovations to create space for the bank at 102 boulevard Haussmann, Proust had moved out as quickly as possible. But as a result of all the veterans who had returned or relocated to postwar Paris, apartments had become scarce. Here is what Proust tells Forssgren in the letter:

> I did not wait for the beginning of the work to flee such disorder, but since it was during the time when it was impossible to find lodging, I came here (first rue L-Pichat), the only apartment vacant then in Paris, but which is horribly ugly and excessively expensive. Your letters probably arrived after my move and were lost. I wish you great luck with your invention, but you

5. "My dear Ernest, It is impossible for me to see you given the short notice that you have given me, therefore, farewell. Cordially yours, Marcel. (PS) If you have to write or phone me send your letter in my name to 44, rue Hamelin."

told me not to talk about it to anyone (besides I don't know what
it is) yet I see that you talk about it.
Believe me your cordially devoted
Marcel Proust[6]

We note that this letter bears the formal "Marcel Proust,"
rather than the more intimate "Marcel" of the note left at the
Riviera Hotel. This letter is presumably the reply to the one that
Forssgren wrote to Proust after receiving the telegram.

Page 355. Painter's paragraph begins, "Early in October, on a
foggy evening, Proust attended a last soirée at the Beaumonts' and returned with a sore throat, which next day became a severe cold."[7] Céleste, perhaps echoing Painter, also
says that Proust caught his cold one October night when he
attended a big party at the Beaumonts'. There is no record of
his having done so. One would expect Forssgren to welcome
this news that exonerates him from being the unwitting
cause of Proust's last illness and death, but he writes in the
margin: "The first stage was brought on by 'The mysterious
visit.' The beginning of the end, his last illness, as the Dr.
said." Here Forssgren is quoting himself from the memoirs
and thus relying on his own memory of the attempt to visit
Proust during the health crisis he depicts as fatal. All the evidence indicates that he cannot have witnessed such a scene.
There is, however, one possible explanation. Assuming that
Forssgren called on Proust in early September, he likely arrived
at 44 rue Hamelin when Proust was suffering from severe

6. *Corr.* 21: 480. We note that Proust does not mention any letters he
wrote to Forssgren after the valet's departure in 1915.

7. Because of his method of referencing, it's difficult to identify Painter's source for this information. Philip Kolb apparently was unable to do so
as well because he gives no indication of Proust's attending this party in the
chronology he established for the letters of 1922.

asthma attacks and was unable to see him. There may have been an atmosphere of crisis in the apartment that Forssgren later magnified in his retelling of it in the memoirs.

What follows is a summary of Proust's health-related activities in 1922, taken directly from his published correspondence. The year had not been a good one overall for his health; a series of accidents weakened the already famously ill Proust. On May 1, while signing, as gifts to his friends, the first hundred copies of *Sodom and Gomorrah,* part 2, Proust decided to take some dry adrenaline in an unusually strong dose. When he swallowed the powder that he had neglected to dilute sufficiently, it severely burned his digestive tract. Howling in pain, he was forced to stop signing the books. This carelessness resulted in days of fevers and the inability to take any solid food.[8]

By May 18 Proust had recovered enough to attend the party hosted by his British friends Sydney and Violet Schiff at the Hotel Majestic, where the famous but brief, inconsequential encounter with James Joyce took place. Among the other guests were Clive Bell, Pablo Picasso, Serge Diaghilev, and Igor Stravinsky, whose ballet *Renard* had premiered that evening and in whose honor the party was given.

During most of the summer, Proust's routine was fairly normal in that he went occasionally to the Ritz Hotel and attended at least one party. On July 15 he dined out with two friends at the Boeuf sur le toit. In early August he broke his reading glasses and did not feel well enough to have them replaced. On August 20 a fire in the chimney in Proust's room nearly asphyxiated the long-suffering asthma patient. He had to leave his room from time to time in search of fresh air, "even at 3. a.m." By September 2 or 3 he was suffering from severe attacks of asthma, and a week later from vertigo. Every time he tried to get out of bed and stand up, he fell to the floor. If Forssgren arrived at 44 rue Hamelin to see Proust shortly after September 2, he would certainly have been turned away.

8. *Corr.* 21: ii.

Based on the evidence then available to him—that is, the undated note left at the Riviera Hotel and the fragment of the photocopied letter of September 19—Philip Kolb placed the "mysterious visit" shortly before September 19. The telegram of September 1 moves the date of the visit back to late August. It is highly probable that Proust, seeking relief from the smell of smoke lingering from the chimney fire, used the opportunity, while out seeking fresh air, to call at the Hotel Riviera, hoping to catch Forssgren in. By September 22 or 23 Dr. Maurice Bize, Proust's regular physician, called on the writer, who was feeling better as a result of taking new medication, "a mixture of evat-mine and Kola," the first of which gave him some relief from his asthma, while the second served to stimulate his heart.[9] Proust prized Bize for his pleasant, reassuring nature and, especially for his lack of interference with Proust's self-medication. Proust once exclaimed to his brother in a letter critical of other overzealous doctors, "Ah! the restfulness of doctors like good old Bize, who hasn't listened to my chest for ten years."[10]

We note that Dr. Bize's visit is just before Forssgren's sailing date, that Proust is enjoying better health, and that his complaints are about his usual asthma and not a cold. By mid-October, his close friend of many years Lucien Daudet called on Proust, but the writer, now suffering from a cold, was too ill to receive him. This fits with a letter in which Proust says he caught a cold in the first part of October, but not at the Beaumonts' party. The source was much closer to home and did involve servants, but not the former Swedish footman.

In this letter, published since Painter's biography and Céleste's memoirs, we find that Proust blamed the infection on Odilon and especially Céleste. Writing to Paul Morand in the first half of November, a short time before his death, Proust explained that he had not been well for a month: "Odilon had caught a cold that lasted only a day, but Céleste, refusing to put

9. *SL* 4: 445 and n. 1.
10. *SL* 4: 157.

on any rhinogomenol [a disinfectant], gave me the cold with a rapidity such that one would have thought she was in a hurry for me to catch it. For a little more than a month I have been reduced to coughing fits, fever, etc., asthma revived from my youth. Alas, youth itself has not revived."[11] Since Proust, who says he has been ill "for a little more than a month," is writing, according to Philip Kolb's determination of the date, during the first half of November, he must have caught the cold from the Albarets during the first two weeks of October, well after Forssgren had sailed from Cherbourg on September 26 or 27, and more than a month after the "mysterious visit." Proust's testimony in this letter supports the other evidence provided by the postmark of the September 1 telegram and the Ellis Island records showing that Forssgren arrived on the *Majestic* in New York City on October 2, 1922.

Once Proust became genuinely concerned about his health, he had Jacques Rivière write to his brother, Dr. Maurice Rivière, who practiced in Bordeaux, to ask him to explain what the presence of pneumococcus portended for him. He asked Jacques to keep the letter secret, a strategy that he saw as necessary because he feared his own brother's intervention.[12] When Proust knew that he had pneumonia, he understood that there was virtually nothing medicine could do to save him, since antibiotics were unavailable then. His body would have to fight off the disease or succumb. In any case, he obstinately refused the advice and pleas of those closest to him—Céleste, his brother Robert, and Reynaldo Hahn—to enter a clinic, where his chances of survival would have been optimized by rest, nourishment, and the best available palliatives. Proust, son and brother of distinguished physicians, had long since lost all faith in medicine to cure his ills. He had long relied on his own arcane theories and strange regimen, and on constant self-medication, primarily sedatives to get to sleep and stimulants to stay awake, including,

11. *Corr.* 21: 531.
12. *Corr.* 21: 511–12, 528.

at times, massive doses of coffee and even caffeine pills. There is even some indication that Proust may have wished to die.[13] Some years earlier he had told Céleste, in a poignant scene, that he could die now that his Herculean labors were finished or nearly so. Here is the scene as Céleste remembered it, when she heard the bell ring one afternoon around four o'clock:

"He'd only rung once, so I went in empty-handed (he would ring twice for the tray). He was resting in bed, his head and shoulders slightly raised on the pillow as usual, with the light of the little lamp leaving his face in the shadow except for the eyes, the look that was always so strong that you felt it watching or following you." She noticed he had not had his fumigation. "He looked very tired, but he smiled at me as I came in. Suddenly I was struck by the radiance of his expression. As I came up to the bed he turned his head slightly toward me, opened his lips, and spoke. It was the first time he'd ever spoken to me immediately . . . before having had his first cup of coffee." He reminded her of "a child who had found the most beautiful toy and the greatest happiness."

He said, "Dear Céleste, I have great news to tell you."
I said, "Well, what? What happened last night in this room that was so important?"
"Something tremendous. Something so wonderful!"
"Well, what happened?"
He sat up in bed, smiled at me and said: "I have written the words 'The End.' Now I can die."
So I said to him, "But what about all the bits of paper I still have to paste together? And all the corrections you still have to make?"
"That, my dear, that's something else."[14]

13. For a description of Proust's last days, see William C. Carter, *Marcel Proust: A Life* (New Haven: Yale University Press, 2000), 799–810.
14. There are two records of Céleste's account of this exciting moment, on film in a 1962 documentary, *Portrait-Souvenir: Marcel Proust,* and in her

Céleste did not want the enchanter to die or to even speak of death.

Proust had written the word *Fin* (The end) and underlined it. Although Céleste, in her memoirs, was certain this extraordinary moment took place in 1922, it probably occurred years earlier, perhaps as early as 1916, when Proust informed his publisher Gaston Gallimard that, in the event of his untimely death, the novel could be published.[15] Why would Proust give Gallimard such an authorization if he had not written the conclusion to his great work? For as long as he lived Proust would expand and revise his manuscripts, but sometime in 1916 or not long afterward, he gave his book its ultimate shape if not its final dimensions.

Perhaps Proust imagined the day of his own burial in a way similar to that of Bergotte, the fictional novelist he created for *In Search of Lost Time:* "They buried him, but all through that night of mourning, in the lighted shop-windows, his books, arranged three by three, kept vigil like angels with outspread wings and seemed, for him who was no more, the symbol of his resurrection."[16]

---

memoirs. In both versions the contents of the conversation with Proust are the same, but the film interview is more lively. I have used both versions here. See Albaret, *Monsieur Proust,* 338–62. Excerpts of Céleste relating this incident and speaking about Proust's health and eating habits can be seen in the 1993 documentary made for American television: *Marcel Proust: A Writer's Life.*

15. *Corr.* 16: 417. It was while attempting to date this event that Céleste wrote she particularly regretted not having kept a diary during the years she was with Proust. Albaret, *Monsieur Proust,* 335.

16. *The Captive* 5: 246.

Index

❖ ❖ ❖